Life Changing Journey

750 Inspirational Quotes

SERIES VIII

"Unveiling Wisdom: Inspiring Quotes to Spark Your Life. A Treasury of Inspiration for Cultivating Positivity on Life, Love, Nature, and More."

SHREE SHAMBAV

Life Changing Journey – Series VIII
750 Inspirational Quotes
Shree Shambav

Published by Shree Shambav, Tamil Nadu, India

All Rights Reserved

First Edition, 2025

Copyright © 2025, Muniswamy Rajakumar

All rights reserved. No part of this publication may be reproduced, distributed, or transmitted in any form or by any means, including photocopying, recording, or other electronic or mechanical methods, without the author's prior written permission. It is illegal to copy this book, post it to a website, or distribute it by any other means without permission.

The request for permission should be addressed to the author.

ISBN: 978-93-343-0293-6

Email:shreeshambav@gmail.com
Web:www.shambav.org

DEDICATION

"Isavasyam idam sarvam yat kim ca jagatyam jagat, tena tyaktena bhunjitha, ma gridhah kasyasvid dhanam"

To the Almighty,

the Divine Masters,

the family who listens,

and my parents who see –

your presence shapes the pages of my life's journey.

"Isavasyam idam sarvam yat kim ca jagatyam jagat"

Meaning: "God encompasses everything you perceive, see, or touch with your sense organs."

DISCLAIMER

This book, *"Life-Changing Journey - Inspirational Quotes: Series VIII,"* is a heartfelt compilation of personal reflections and insights born from the author's journey of understanding life and the natural world. Each inspirational quote is a subjective truth—a distillation of experience and thought—meant to serve as a mirror for readers to explore their own perspectives and uncover meaning through the lens of their unique experiences.

The intention behind this book is to share a message imbued with compassion, love, and care. It is designed to inspire readers on their personal journeys and guide them toward discovering the deeper realities of life. This is not a prescriptive manual but an invitation to pause, reflect, and engage with life's profound yet simple truths.

It's important to acknowledge that neither the content nor the sequence of the quotes is intended to cause harm, discomfort, or conflict with the reader's personal beliefs. Should any part of the book feel unsettling or contradictory to one's convictions, it is purely coincidental and never intentional.

The journey through these quotes is one of openness and fluidity, free from rigid interpretations or dogmatic assertions. The content reflects the author's personal perspective, humbly offered as a source of inspiration and gentle guidance. Readers are invited to engage with the material at their own pace, to reflect deeply, and to adapt the wisdom within to align with their inner truths and life experiences.

Above all, this book aspires to spark joy, nurture connection, and encourage purposeful living. It gently beckons readers to cultivate a life rooted in compassion, integrity, and intentionality while embracing the beauty of each moment with grace and mindfulness. May the words within these pages illuminate your path as you embark on a transformative journey of self-discovery, growth, and renewal. The journey is uniquely yours, and it is an honour for the author to accompany you, even if only in spirit, as you navigate the unfolding of your life.

With this understanding, readers are encouraged to approach the book with an open mind and heart, recognising that its wisdom is offered not as universal truth but as a collection of insights shaped by the author's personal experiences. You are invited to absorb what resonates, reinterpret what feels unfamiliar, and find your own meaning within these words.

Ultimately, the author's deepest wish is that these reflections serve as a beacon of hope, a source of motivation, and a catalyst for positivity as you embark on your life-changing journey. May this book inspire you to walk your path with courage, grace, and an unwavering belief in the beauty of life's unfolding.

Note - If any part of the book, in any sequence, hurts the reader's sentiments, it would be just out of a sheer accident, not intentional

Divine

"In the tender embrace of surrender lies a profound revelation—the raw, unspoken beauty of union. Each ripple of the river becomes a whispered confession, a declaration of belonging to something greater than itself. As the river flows ceaselessly, unveiling its eternal unity with the boundless ocean, so too does the soul, in its sacred act of surrender, unveil its timeless connection to the Divine.

This surrender is not a loss but a metamorphosis of unparalleled grace, where the fragmented self dissolves into the infinite. And in that dissolution, the soul discovers the ineffable depth of its true essence—a profound oneness with the Divine, unbroken and eternal. It is a sacred symphony, an eternal melody that reverberates through the very fabric of existence, calling us back to the home we never truly left."

– Shree Shambav

EPIGRAM

"In every quiet moment lies a truth, in every tear, a teaching, and in every heartbeat, a sacred whisper. This is not just a book of quotes—it is a mirror of the soul, reflecting the beauty, fragility, and resilience of the human journey."

– Shree Shambav

Life Changing Journey

750 Inspirational Quotes

Shree Shambav

Shree Shambav is a 37x best-selling author renowned for his transformative works in personal development and spiritual growth.

Dear Cherished Readers

Dear Cherished Readers,

As I embark on this new literary voyage, my heart swells with profound gratitude and an overwhelming sense of connection. With deep emotion, I extend my heartfelt appreciation to each of you who has joined me on this journey.

With sincere warmth, I invite you to revisit the steps we have taken together through the pages of my earlier works. Our odyssey began with "Journey of Soul - Karma," a book that marked my first foray into the world of words and a testament to the raw passion that ignited my writing adventure.

The subsequent chapters of our shared narrative unfolded through the enchanting tapestry of the "Twenty + One" series. Each page turned was a brushstroke on the canvas of our imaginations, painting vivid stories that I hoped would resonate deeply within your hearts.

And how can I forget the transformative journey we embarked on with the "Life Changing Journey -

Inspirational Quotes Series." Day by day, quote by quote, we delved into reflections that uplifted, inspired, and sought to bring a glimpse of light to our souls.

The release of "Death - Light of Life and the Shadow of Death" promises to shed new light on the timeless mystery of death.

The **Optimum Python Series** is a comprehensive guide designed to empower readers at every stage of their programming journey. It begins with *Series I: Ultimate Guide for Beginners*, which lays a strong foundation in Python, making it accessible and engaging for newcomers. *Series II: Exploring Data Structures and Algorithms* takes the next step, offering a deep dive into core computer science principles that enhance problem-solving skills and coding efficiency. Building on this, *Series III: Python Power for Data Science* introduces powerful libraries such as NumPy, Pandas, Matplotlib, and Scikit-learn, guiding readers through data manipulation, visualisation, and foundational machine learning techniques. Finally, *Series IV: Unleashing the Potential of Data Science with Machine Learning Techniques* explores advanced machine learning models and real-world applications, enabling readers to harness the full potential of data-driven insights. Whether you're just starting out or looking to master sophisticated tools and strategies, this series is your roadmap to Python proficiency and beyond.

Shree Shambav expands his artistic repertoire with *"Whispers of Eternity: 150 Plus - A Symphony of Soulful Verses,"* a heartfelt exploration of the human experience. Alongside this, his *"Whispers of the Soul: A Journey Through Haiku"* distils profound insights into poignant verses. Together, these works showcase his versatility and mastery of soulful expression, inviting readers on a journey of self-discovery. Through his poetry, he weaves a rich tapestry of emotion that resonates deeply with the heart.

Shree Shambav's latest works—*Learn to Love Yourself: A Journey of Discovering Inner Beauty and Strength Through 10 Transformative Rules, The Power of Letting Go: Embrace Freedom and Happiness, A Journey of Lasting Peace*—are true *treasures of self-discovery, The Entitlement Trap: Get Over It, Get On, Whispers of a Dying Soul: Unspoken Regrets and Unlived Dreams, Whispers of Silence - Unlocking Inner Power through Stillness, The Power of Words: Transforming Speech, Transforming Lives, The Art of Intentional Living: Minimalism for a Life of Purpose, Awakening the Infinite:The Power of Consciousness in Transforming Life, Beyond the Veil: A Journey Through Life After Death series, Bonds Beyond Blood - Where love builds bridges, and bonds defy blood., A Journey into Spiritual Maturity - 12 Golden Rules for Inner Transformation, The Seeker's Gold: Unlocking Life's Greatest Treasure and The Power of Manifestation - Unlocking The Path From Thought To Reality.*

In addition to these works, Shree Shambav has recently ventured into astrology with the release of

Astrology Unveiled – Foundations of Ancient Wisdom Series I to VIII, expanding into the realm of metaphysics. These books explore the foundational principles of Vedic astrology, offering readers a rich and practical understanding of this ancient wisdom.

Your unwavering support, enthusiasm to immerse yourself in my writings, and readiness to embark on these journeys with me have been my greatest sources of inspiration. Your input has been a beacon guiding me through the creation process, moulding these stories into containers of passion, emotion, knowledge, and resonance.

As I unveil this new narrative before you, know that your presence, insights, and shared moments have been my companions. The path we have walked together is etched in the annals of my creative evolution, and it's an honour beyond words to have you by my side once more.

Here's to the readers who have illuminated my path with their presence, who have embraced my stories with open hearts, and who have woven themselves into the very fabric of my literary world. Our journey has been a symbiotic dance of writer and reader, a harmony of souls brought together by the magic of storytelling.

With a heart brimming with appreciation and eyes glistening with anticipation, I extend my deepest gratitude for your unwavering support. Thank you for the memories, the shared emotions, and the countless hours spent in the worlds we've crafted together. As we step into this new adventure, let's continue to explore, feel, and discover the boundless horizons that words can unveil.

Warmly,

Shree Shambav

SHREE SHAMBAV

Suggested Reads

FROM BEST-SELLING AUTHOR

Endorsements

"Life-Changing Journey – Inspirational Quotes Series" is more than a collection of inspiring words—it is a heartfelt companion for those navigating the sacred path of self-discovery, healing, and transformation. In this soul-stirring volume, Shree Shambav masterfully blends profound wisdom with poetic elegance, offering reflections that resonate with the very core of our being. Each quote feels like a sacred whisper from the universe—a quiet reminder of our inner resilience, our divine essence, and the grace that lies in simply being human. This is not just a book to be read—it's one to be lived with. A source of light in moments of darkness, a guide when the road feels uncertain, and a friend to turn to for clarity, comfort, and strength. A timeless companion for the soul.

- UMA Devi (Entrepreneur)

About the Author

Shree Shambav is an internationally acclaimed, best-selling author, inspirational speaker, artist, philanthropist, life coach, and entrepreneur. A world record holder, his deep passion for music led him to create soul-stirring albums, drawing inspiration from his celebrated poetry collection, Whispers of Eternity. His profound insights have sparked deep personal transformations, guiding countless individuals toward self-discovery, purposeful living, and authenticity.

With an extraordinary ability to unlock human potential, Shree empowers individuals to break through limitations and embrace their highest selves. His writings, lectures, and compassionate guidance continue to uplift lives, fostering resilience, mindfulness, and personal growth.

Shree Shambav is a 37x best-selling author celebrated for his profound contributions to personal development and spiritual growth.

Shree Shambav's literary journey took flight with the celebrated Journey of Soul - Karma, where he delved into the depths of human experience to unveil profound insights. Garnering recognition through multiple literature awards, his repertoire includes esteemed works, such as the Twenty + One Series and the enlightening Life Changing Journey series.

As a distinguished alumnus of the Indian Institute of Management and the National Institute of Technology, Shree Shambav brings a wealth of corporate acumen from his tenure in multinational corporations. His most recent publications, including Unveiling the Enigma, Death - Light of Life and the Shadow of Death and Optimum - Python Series I, Series II, Series III and Series IV, demonstrate his mastery of both the literary and technical spheres.

Shree Shambav expands his artistic repertoire with *"Whispers of Eternity: 150 Plus - A Symphony of Soulful Verses,"* a heartfelt exploration of the human experience. Alongside this, his *"Whispers of the Soul: A Journey Through Haiku"* distils profound insights into poignant verses. Together, these works showcase his versatility and mastery of soulful expression, inviting readers on a journey of self-discovery. Through his poetry, he weaves a rich tapestry of emotion that resonates deeply with the heart.

Shree Shambav's latest works—*Learn to Love Yourself: A Journey of Discovering Inner Beauty and Strength Through 10 Transformative Rules, The Power of Letting Go: Embrace Freedom and Happiness, A Journey of Lasting Peace*—are true *treasures of self-discovery, The Entitlement Trap: Get Over It, Get On, Whispers of a Dying Soul: Unspoken Regrets and Unlived Dreams, Whispers of Silence - Unlocking Inner Power through Stillness, The Power of Words: Transforming Speech, Transforming Lives, The Art of Intentional Living: Minimalism for a Life of Purpose, Awakening the Infinite:The Power of Consciousness in Transforming Life, Beyond the Veil: A Journey Through Life After Death series, Bonds Beyond Blood - Where love builds bridges, and bonds defy blood., A Journey into Spiritual Maturity - 12 Golden Rules for Inner Transformation, The Seeker's Gold: Unlocking Life's Greatest Treasure and The Power of Manifestation - Unlocking The Path From Thought To Reality.*

In addition to these works, Shree Shambav has recently ventured into astrology with the release of Astrology Unveiled – Foundations of Ancient Wisdom Series I to VIII, expanding into the realm of metaphysics. These books explore the foundational principles of Vedic astrology, offering readers a rich and practical understanding of this ancient wisdom.

Shree Shambav established the Ayur Rakshita Foundation, which is dedicated to promoting boundless growth, universal fraternity, and environmental protection. The charity helps diverse communities while working for societal progress.

To learn more about Shree Shambav and his works, visit his website at www.shambav.org. For information about the Ayur Rakshita Foundation and its initiatives, visit www.shambav-ayurrakshita.org.

Let's Follow him on Social Media: **@shreeshambav**

Main: https://linktr.ee/shreeshambav

Website: https://www.shambav.org/

LinkedIn: https://www.linkedin.com/in/shreeshambav/

Blog: https://blog.shambav.org/

Instagram: https://www.instagram.com/shreeshambav/

YouTube: https://www.youtube.com/@shreeshambav

Amazon: https://www.amazon.com/author/shreeshambav

Goodreads: https://www.goodreads.com/author/show/22367436.Shree_Shambav

PREFACE

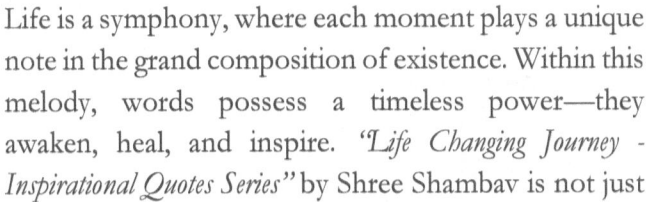

Life is a symphony, where each moment plays a unique note in the grand composition of existence. Within this melody, words possess a timeless power—they awaken, heal, and inspire. *"Life Changing Journey - Inspirational Quotes Series"* by Shree Shambav is not just a collection of phrases; it is a companion, a guide, and a beacon for those navigating the intricate pathways of life.

This book was conceived in the quiet spaces where inspiration is born—in those still moments when the noise of the world fades and the soul begins to speak. Every quote in this collection distils universal truths into simple yet profound expressions, echoing the essence of human experience. Through these pages, you are invited to embark on a journey of self-discovery, reflection, and transformation.

The chapters are thoughtfully crafted, each offering a thematic exploration of the human spirit. They illuminate the courage required to embrace change, the resilience to chase dreams, and the wisdom to find meaning amid life's adversities. They delve into love and relationships, the beauty of self-acceptance, and the quiet strength that lies dormant within. These chapters whisper of joy found in simplicity, gratitude awakened through mindfulness, and the profound connection we share with the natural world and the cosmos.

This book is a tapestry woven with timeless insights that transcend circumstances. It invites you to pause, reflect, and draw inspiration from the wellspring of human wisdom. Whether you are weathering life's storms, seeking the motivation to pursue your aspirations, or yearning for the serenity of inner peace, these quotes serve as a trusted guide and confidant.

In Series III, themes like *"Embracing Change," "Discovering Self," "Dreams and Aspirations," "Embracing Imperfections," "Finding Inner Strength,"* and *"Gratitude and Mindfulness"* invite you to reflect on identity, purpose, and the pursuit of your passions.

Series IV delves deeper into *"Inspiration and Motivation," "Lessons from Adversity," "Love and Relationships," "Nature's Symphony," "Pursuing Your Dreams,"* and *"Serenity and Balance"*—nurturing connections, fostering resilience, and celebrating life's harmony.

Series V culminates in the profound, with themes like *"Shades of Existence," "Success and Achievement," "The Beauty of Simplicity," "The Power of Kindness,"* and *"Wisdom from the Ages."* These chapters remind us to cherish the beauty in life's simplest moments and draw strength from timeless truths.

Series VI culminates in a journey of inner stillness and soulful reflection, exploring themes such as *"Embracing Change," "Love and Relationships," "Serenity and Balance," "Shades of Existence,"* and *"Whispers of the Divine."* Each chapter gently invites us to slow down, to find meaning in silence, and to recognise the sacred in everyday life. They are reminders that life's simplest moments often carry the most profound truths and that true strength arises when we listen deeply—to others, to nature, and to our hearts.

Series VII deepens this introspection, guiding us through themes like *"Discovering the Self," "Finding Inner Strength," "Lessons from Adversity," "The Power of Kindness,"* and *"Wisdom from the Ages."*

Series VIII invites readers on a deeper path of introspection, embracing themes like change, imperfections, and inner strength.

Rooted in mindfulness, gratitude, and inspiration, it nurtures quiet resilience and clarity.

Through nature's rhythms and life's simple truths, it gently reminds us that lasting transformation begins within.

These chapters serve as lanterns on the path of growth—illuminating how hardship refines us, how kindness transforms, and how the wisdom of those who walked before us still echoes with relevance today. They remind us that every challenge holds a lesson, and every moment offers a choice to awaken.

Shree Shambav's words transcend the mundane, touching the sacred essence of life. They serve as gentle reminders of our shared humanity, encouraging us to embrace imperfections and live authentically. Each quote is a spark—a catalyst for growth and self-discovery, illuminating the path through life's trials and triumphs.

As you turn these pages, may you find not just words but a profound connection to your inner self and the world around you. Let this collection be a sanctuary of wisdom, a reservoir of courage, and a wellspring of inspiration, empowering you to embrace life with an open heart and an awakened soul.

Welcome to the *"Life Changing Journey - Inspirational Quotes Series."* May this book inspire you to live boldly, love deeply, and discover the boundless joy within your own journey.

LIFE CHANGING JOURNEY

Let the journey unfold.

With gratitude and encouragement,

Shree Shambav

INTRODUCTION

In a world that often feels like a whirlwind of expectations, responsibilities, and endless noise, it's easy to lose sight of the deeper meaning of life. We rush through our days, chasing goals and ticking off to-do lists, yet many of us long for something more—something that grounds us, inspires us, and reconnects us to the beauty of existence.

This longing is the seed from which the *"Life Changing Journey - Inspirational Quotes Series"* was born. At its heart, this book is an invitation—a gentle call to pause, reflect, and rediscover the wisdom that lies within and around us.

Words have an extraordinary ability to shape our perspectives and transform our lives. A single phrase encountered at the right moment can shift our understanding, provide clarity in times of confusion, or ignite a spark of courage in the face of fear. This collection of quotes was curated with this transformative power in mind. Each one is a distillation of universal truths designed to speak directly to the soul and awaken the resilience, hope, and strength that reside within us all.

This book unfolds as a journey through a series of reflections, each thoughtfully curated to illuminate the many dimensions of the human experience.

Series VIII deepens the journey of introspection, guiding readers through profound themes such as embracing change, accepting imperfections, and discovering inner strength. With reflections rooted in gratitude, mindfulness, and inspiration, this collection awakens a quiet resilience and renewed perspective. It celebrates the symphony of nature, the subtle shades of existence, and the beauty found in simplicity—offering a gentle yet powerful reminder that transformation begins within.

Through these reflections, you will uncover the resilience to navigate life's transitions, the courage to embrace your authentic self, and the joy of living with gratitude. Each theme is a stepping stone, leading you closer to understanding the beauty of imperfection and the strength that lies within.

As you journey through these pages, you will traverse a rich tapestry of themes that reflect the multifaceted nature of life. From the courage required to embrace change to the wisdom found in adversity, the tenderness of nurturing love and relationships, and the quiet strength discovered in gratitude and simplicity—each chapter serves as a portal to deeper self-reflection and understanding.

This series is not just a collection of words but a companion for your personal growth, offering profound insights that encourage you to live authentically and harmoniously.

But this book is not meant to be read in a rush. It is not a novel to be consumed from cover to cover in one sitting. Instead, it is a companion for life's journey, offering guidance and solace whenever you need it most. You might find comfort in a quote during a moment of despair, draw courage from a phrase when facing a challenge, or uncover a fresh perspective as you navigate a crossroads.

The beauty of this collection lies in its timelessness. Whether you're at the beginning of your journey, in the midst of transformation, or reflecting on lessons learned, these quotes will meet you where you are. They are not answers but mirrors, reflecting the wisdom you already possess and encouraging you to trust your inner voice.

We live in a time where the external world demands so much of us, yet the most profound answers often come from within. This book is a reminder to listen to that quiet voice—the one that whispers truths when the world falls silent. It is a guide to help you realign with your authentic self, find purpose amidst uncertainty, and celebrate the beauty of being alive.

As you turn the pages of this book, my hope is that you discover not just inspiration but a renewed sense of connection—to yourself, to others, and to the world around you. Let these quotes be your compass, pointing you toward a life of greater meaning, joy, and fulfilment.

This journey is yours to take. With each quote, may you find the courage to embrace your unique path and the wisdom to live it fully.

Welcome to the *"Life Changing Journey - Inspirational Quotes Series."* May these words guide you toward the light within and inspire you to create a life that resonates with your truest self.

With love and gratitude,

Warm regards,

Shree Shambav

PROLOGUE

In the hush of a still moment—when the world's clamor softens and the endless doing gives way to quiet being—something sacred stirs. It is not in the towering milestones that life's deepest truths are measured but in the soft, almost imperceptible whispers of wisdom that arise in the spaces between. These whispers do not shout. They do not arrive with thunder. Instead, they emerge gently—wrapped in the ache of letting go, the warmth of shared laughter, the sting of heartbreak, and the silent strength of rising once more.

They come to us not as grand revelations but as flickers—fragments of truth carried in the wind, woven into the fabric of our everyday lives. A tear shed in solitude, a hand held in silence, a dream rekindled after despair—each becomes a sacred messenger, echoing something eternal. These moments are not just experiences; they are soul-invitations. Each one calls us to return to ourselves, to remember what we've forgotten, and to honour the quiet depth of our humanity.

This book is a collection of such whispers.

It is not a guidebook nor a prescription. It does not claim to have answers. Rather, it offers reflections—like stars scattered across a night sky—small lights that might help illuminate the terrain of your inner world. Every quote within these pages has been born from lived experience and quiet contemplation, from raw emotion and hard-won clarity. They are not written *to* you, but *for* you—for the part of you that longs to feel seen, understood, and gently awakened.

The inspiration behind this book did not arrive in a single epiphany. It came through the patient unfolding of life itself—in moments of stillness, in the quiet aftermath of grief, in the tender awe of nature, and in the sacred conversations held between the soul and the stars. The universe, it seems, speaks most clearly when we finally stop to listen.

Because life is not a linear path—it is a spiral of remembering. A mosaic of broken pieces made beautiful by the light that shines through the cracks. It is a dance between chaos and grace, between pain and peace, between losing ourselves and finding something far deeper than we imagined.

This book is an invitation to pause. To breathe. To return.

To that space within you that holds your truest knowing—the one that survives the noise, the expectations, and the fears. It is for the dreamers who yearn for something more, the seekers who walk through shadow in search of light, and the quiet warriors who carry their questions like sacred flames.

As you turn these pages, may you find echoes of your own story—the parts that hurt, the parts that healed, and the parts still becoming. These words are not tied to any one voice or journey. They are a chorus of our shared humanity. They remind us that even when we feel most alone, we are part of something vast, interconnected, and divinely unfolding.

This is not just a book—it is a companion for the soul. A flicker of warmth in moments of cold. A hand extended through the pages. A mirror reflecting back the beauty, resilience, and radiant truth that already lives inside you.

Welcome to *The Life-Changing Journey – Inspirational Quotes Series.*

With reverence, with hope, and with love,
– Shree Shambav

CONTENTS

DEDICATION iii

DISCLAIMER v

Divine ix

EPIGRAM xi

Dear Cherished Readers xv

Suggested Reads xx

Endorsements xxi

About the Author xxiii

PREFACE xxvii

INTRODUCTION xxxiii

PROLOGUE xxxvii

Embracing Change 1
   Navigating Life's Transformations 1

Embracing Imperfections 33
   Embracing Self-Acceptance 33

Finding Inner Strength 67
   Empowering the Mind and Spirit 67

Gratitude and Mindfulness 103
   Finding Joy in the Present 103

Inspiration and Motivation 139
   Fuelling the Soul 139

Nature Symphony 175
   Odes to the Earth 175
Shades of Existence 195
   Light of life 195
The Beauty of Simplicity 231
   Embracing Life's Little Pleasures 231
Life Coach and Philanthropist 265
TESTIMONIALS 269
ACKNOWLEDGEMENTS 279

Embracing Change

Navigating Life's Transformations

"You are not meant to resist the current, but to become the river. Every twist, every turn, every fall—each is shaping you into the vast ocean of your becoming."

- *Shree Shambav*

Alignment Over Effort

"The universe moves not by force, but by flow — align with its rhythm, and manifestation becomes a dance, not a struggle."

Becoming the Flow

"You are not meant to resist the current, but to become the river. Every twist, every turn, every fall—each is shaping you into the vast ocean of your becoming."

Between Cause and Becoming

"Your life is not a sentence passed by fate, but a space between cause and becoming — shaped by choice."

Beyond the Mind's Horizon

"To manifest is not to chase — it is to dissolve the distance between who you are and what already seeks you."

Brushstrokes of Becoming

"Each thought, each choice, is a brushstroke. Paint not with fear or longing, but with clarity and soul."

Dreams with Roots

"A dream without action is a wish. A dream with aligned action is a seed taking root in reality."

Echoes of Emotion

"Emotion is not reaction — it is vibration. What you feel consistently is what you summon into your space."

Echoes of the Divine

"Every leaf that dances in the breeze, every mountain that stands in silence, speaks a language of reverence. The Earth is an eternal ode, reminding us that we are part of something much greater than ourselves."

Echoes of the Unspoken

"Some truths are not taught—they arrive in the hush between breaths, when the heart is finally still enough to listen."

Elegance in the Ordinary

"Simplicity is not the absence of richness, but the presence of clarity. It is in the quiet moments of stillness, the unspoken joys, that we uncover the profound beauty of life."

Embracing the Now

"In the quiet stillness of the present moment, we find the vast expanse of eternity. Mindfulness is the art of stepping into the now, where joy is not a destination, but a way of being."

Emotion is Energy in Prayer

"Every emotion is a prayer wrapped in vibration — answered not by words, but by the resonance it creates within and around you."

Emotional Alchemy

"Unexamined emotions are like hidden rivers beneath the surface — they shape the landscape of your life without ever asking permission."

Freedom from the Invisible Cage

"Most cages are built not of iron, but of unseen beliefs. To change your life, first find the keys within."

Frequency of Faith

"Faith is not blind; it is the subtle knowing that your vibration has already reached what your eyes have yet to see."

From Force to Flow

"Manifestation is not born of force but flow—not of grasping, but of gentle surrender with unwavering trust."

From Passive to Powerful

"Manifestation begins the moment you stop wishing for life to happen, and start vibrating as if it already has."

From Trying to Trusting

"Trying is the path of the mind; trusting is the doorway of the heart."

Grace Wears Quiet Feet

"Transformation doesn't always announce itself—it tiptoes in as grace, just after you've let go of control."

Gratitude in the Smallest Things

"In the gentle breeze, a warm cup of tea, or the smile of a stranger, lies the essence of joy. Life's little pleasures are the treasures that, when noticed, make the ordinary extraordinary."

Illuminating the Soul

"The light we seek is not outside of us, but within. It is the quiet brilliance of our spirit, revealing the truth that the brightest flame often begins as a single, humble spark."

In the Pause, the Truth

"Sometimes, the most sacred teachings are not spoken—they're found in the silence Guruji leaves behind."

Intention in Motion

"An intention without action is like a star without light — beautiful, but invisible."

Listening to the Invisible

"The universe speaks in patterns, not paragraphs. Pay attention not to the noise, but to the nudges."

Manifestation Is Not Magic

"Manifestation isn't about asking the universe for more — it's about becoming the version of you who's ready to receive it."

Manifestation Is Resonance

"The universe does not grant wishes; it mirrors frequencies. Manifestation is less about asking and more about becoming."

Manifestation as Memory

"Sometimes we don't manifest to receive something new—we manifest to remember who we already are."

Not to Fix, But to Feel

"Healing begins the moment you stop trying to fix your pain and simply allow yourself to feel it."

Presence Over Power

"It is not the strength of our will, but the depth of our presence, that moves the cosmos to respond."

Resonance Over Request

"The universe responds not to pleading, but to frequency. You attract not what you ask for, but what you embody."

Roots Before Wings

"You cannot bloom into love and abundance unless you first root yourself in self-worth."

Sacred Conversations

"Manifestation is not a command — it is a dialogue between the seen and the unseen, the self and the source."

Seed and Sky

"A single aligned thought, planted in the stillness of belief, carries the weight of galaxies in motion."

Seeds of Now

"The future does not bloom from desire alone — it blossoms from the seeds sown in the now."

Stillness Speaks

"When the noise fades and the mind surrenders, manifestation arises from the silence where the Divine whispers."

Stillness as Source

"In silence, the soul remembers — that before creation begins, there is always a breath, a pause, a sacred stillness."

Tending the Invisible

"Every act of nurturing something outside is a rehearsal for healing something within."

The Alchemy of Awareness

"When karma is met with awareness, it ceases to be repetition and becomes transformation."

The Alchemy of Belief

"Belief is the fire that transforms invisible dreams into tangible destiny."

The Alchemy of Thought

"When belief shifts, suffering dissolves, creativity awakens, and life transforms — not by force, but by the alchemy of inner truth."

The Architecture of Destiny

"Your beliefs are the blueprint, your emotions the mortar, and your choices the bricks — your life is the home you've built, moment by moment."

The Beauty in the Broken

"It is not in perfection that we are most human, but in the cracks where our truth shows. Every flaw is a brushstroke on the masterpiece of your becoming."

The Breath of Liberation

"Each time you breathe out an old belief, you make space for a new reality to be born."

The Bridge Within

"Belief is the bridge between thought and reality; mend the bridge, and your dreams will find their way across."

The Circle that Never Broke

"Separation was the dream; connection is the truth. You have always been held within a circle that never broke."

The Dance of Being

"You are not the fleeting clouds of your emotions; you are the vast sky that cradles them — unchanging, infinite, free."

The Dance of Frequencies

"You do not attract what you desire — you attract what you are in vibration, moment by moment."

The Dance of Shadows and Light

"Life is a canvas painted with both light and shadow. It is in embracing the contrast that we understand the true depth of our existence, for without darkness, the light would have no shape."

The Echo of Integrity

"When your thoughts, words, and actions sing the same song, the Universe becomes your silent choir."

The Echo of Your Inner World

"Reality does not reflect what you desire; it echoes what you believe."

The Edge of Awakening

"There comes a moment, between breath and thought, where the dreamer awakens as the creator."

The Engine of the Will

"Motivation is the engine that powers our will to move beyond limitations. It is the unwavering belief that we are capable of achieving more, not because the world is perfect, but because we are determined to make it so."

The Essence Beneath Pain

"Pain peels away the layers of illusion, carving from within the sculpture of your truest self."

The Fire Within

"Strength isn't forged in ease, but in the quiet moments when you refuse to give up. The fiercest power is the one that rises when no one is watching."

The Fire Within Intention

"Intention is not wishful thinking — it is focused energy that, when aligned with clarity and truth, carves reality like water shapes stone."

The Fire Within the Mirror

"Manifestation does not begin with desire—it begins with the reflection we dare to face within ourselves."

The Fire of Aligned Action

"Manifestation is not wishful thinking — it is sacred movement in the direction of your highest truth."

The Furnace of Identity

"The reality you live in is forged not in external events, but in the silent furnace of your self-concept."

The Gentle Unfolding

"Healing is not a rush to fix the broken, but a slow remembering that you were never broken at all."

The Grace in Letting Go

"Change does not ask for your permission—it invites your surrender. In letting go of what was, you make space for what can be, and that is where true freedom begins."

The Heart of Endurance

"You are not the wound nor the stumble; you are the ancient spirit within, vast and unmoving, waiting to be remembered."

The Hidden Architect

"Behind every outcome in your life stands a belief — silent, unseen, but endlessly powerful."

The Language of the Invisible

"The universe does not speak in sentences, but in synchronicities — listen not with ears, but with alignment."

The Law of Subtle Echoes

"What you whisper in your thoughts today will thunder in the valleys of your tomorrow."

The Lens of Possibility

"Your beliefs are not reflections of truth; they are the lenses through which truth is either distorted or revealed."

The Light We Forgot

"You are not here to earn the light. You are here to remember that you have always been made of it."

The Light You Chase Is You

"Stop chasing the light outside. The day you realise you are the flame, the world begins to glow in your presence."

The Map and the Horizon

"Your beliefs are the maps you carry. Change the map, and new horizons will rise to meet your steps."

The Mirror Within

"The world reflects not who you are, but who you believe yourself to be—change the mirror, and the image shifts."

The Mirror of Becoming

"The world around you is not a place you merely live in — it is a mirror patiently reflecting who you believe you are becoming."

The Mirror of Becoming

"Your outer world is not a reflection of your desires — it is a reflection of your beliefs. Change the lens, and the landscape transforms."

The Mirror of Manifestation

"The Universe does not give you what you want — it gives you what you are aligned with. Change your inner landscape, and the world will echo your transformation."

The Music of Life

"The earth sings in whispers and roars, a melody composed by the winds, rivers, and trees. In its symphony, we find not only the rhythm of life, but the heartbeat of all existence."

The Quiet Departure

"When a master leaves the room in silence, the teachings do not end—they deepen into your bones."

The Rooted Soul

"When you anchor yourself to the unshakable truth within, no winds, no falls, no storms can uproot you."

The Sacred Observer

"The moment you become the observer of your thoughts, rather than their prisoner, you begin to create rather than repeat."

The Sacred Pause

"Sometimes, the universe waits for your stillness — not to slow you down, but to remind you that your presence is the most powerful magnet of all."

The Sacred Realignment

"Every time you realign your beliefs with your soul's truth, the entire universe bends just slightly in your favor."

The Sacred Return

"In every fall, there lies an invitation — not to despair, but to return to the quiet place where you are whole."

The Sacred Thread

"Every thought is a thread; every action is a stitch. Your life is the tapestry you are weaving — with presence or without."

The Sculptor Within

"You are both the marble and the sculptor — karma gives you the shape, manifestation gives you the chisel."

The Seed of Abundance

"Gratitude is not just a feeling; it is the very soil from which abundance grows. In acknowledging the blessings, we sow the seeds of joy, cultivating a harvest that nourishes our soul."

The Silent Communion

"In the silent spaces between thoughts, you are already in communion with everything that ever was and ever will be."

The Silent Sculptor

"Beliefs are silent sculptors — they carve the unseen, and the unseen becomes the life you live."

The Silent Sculptor

"Every thought chisels reality like an invisible hand carving stone — slowly, patiently, with sacred precision."

The Silent Strength

"A rock does not fight the storm; it endures it. True strength is not in resisting life's trials, but in remaining unbroken through them."

The Spark Within

"Inspiration is the spark that awakens the dormant fire within. It does not push us forward; it illuminates the path, reminding us that the journey is just as vital as the destination."

The Story Beneath the Ashes

"Behind every tear and tremble lies a story not of weakness, but of becoming."

The Unseen Sculpture

"Life's hardships are not punishments, but the hands of a divine sculptor, shaping the unseen masterpiece inside you."

The Weaver Within

"Reality is not something you walk into — it's something you weave, thread by thread, with the loom of awareness."

The Weight of Worthiness

"You cannot manifest a life you believe you are unworthy of; the universe responds not to your words, but to your self-regard."

The Wellspring of Creation

"When belief and soul flow as one river, creation is no longer a struggle — it is a song."

The Whisper of the Eternal

"Amid the noise of suffering, listen closely — the eternal within you is always whispering, 'Stand tall, you are made of forever.'"

Threads of Continuity

"Karma threads the past into the present, while manifestation. Rebirth Through Intention: "You don't have to wait for lifetimes to be reborn. Each conscious intention is a resurrection of the soul's truth."

Undoing the Knot

"Limiting beliefs are not chains but knots — with patience and awareness, they can be undone."

Unshakable Roots

"True strength is not loud or seen—it is the calm beneath chaos, the faith that does not waver, and the spirit that bends but never breaks."

Waves in the Field

"Every intention you hold is a ripple in the quantum field — it doesn't ask if you believe, it reflects what you believe."

Whole, Even in Pieces

"You were never meant to be flawless—only fully you. To accept your imperfections is not weakness, but the bravest act of loving who you truly are."

Wholeness Before Witness

"You are not here to become perfect for the world. You are here to remember you are already whole—and let the world witness that light."

Your Inner Frequency

"Manifestation is not about asking — it's about becoming. You don't attract what you want. You attract what you are in harmony with."

Embracing Imperfections

Embracing Self-Acceptance

"It is not in perfection that we are most human, but in the cracks where our truth shows. Every flaw is a brushstroke on the masterpiece of your becoming."

- *Shree Shambav*

Becoming on Purpose

"Purpose is not something you chase—it is what unfolds when you dare to live in alignment with your truth, even when the world misunderstands your path."

Beyond the Mind's Edges

"Your mind builds fences, but your soul is sky—limitless, eternal, and waiting to be remembered."

Beyond the Voice of Fear

"The echoes of fear may linger, but they are no match for the stillness where love begins to sing."

Clearing the Lens

"To see someone clearly, you must first wipe away the smudges of bias from your own lens."

Echoes Through Time

"Wisdom is not bound by age or era—it is the soul's remembering. The truths whispered by sages still breathe in our modern chaos, waiting to be heard beneath the noise."

Echoes of Thought

"Every thought is an echo you send into the cosmos—it always returns, carrying the energy you gave it."

Faith is a Frequency

"Faith is not a belief—it is the vibration you hold when reason is silent and your heart still chooses to trust."

Freedom Through Connection

"The moment we let go of judgment, we free ourselves to love, empathise, and truly connect."

Freedom in Forgiveness

"Forgiveness is not about letting someone off the hook—it's about setting your own soul free from the weight it was never meant to carry."

From Criticism to Curiosity

"When you replace criticism with curiosity, the walls of separation crumble, and the seeds of connection take root."

Grace in the Grind

"Even in your smallest struggles, grace is quietly shaping the architecture of your becoming."

Grace in the Storm

"Inner strength is not the absence of struggle, but the quiet resolve to rise each time you fall. It is the whisper of your soul reminding you that every storm carries the seed of transformation."

Gratitude as a Portal

"Gratitude is the frequency where the door to the miraculous begins to open."

Healing Through Words

"In every conversation lies a choice: to wound with your words or to heal with your heart."

Healing is Not Loud

"Healing often comes not in triumph, but in the quiet moments when love wraps itself around old sorrow."

Hearts Shaped by Care

"It's not brilliance or wealth that shapes hearts; it's the warmth of genuine care and the willingness to stand by someone when they need it most."

Honouring Complexity

"To judge another is to deny their complexity; to understand them is to honour their story."

Invisible Threads

"What you seek is already seeking you, connected by threads of energy no eye can see but every soul can feel."

Letting Go to Let In

"The universe cannot fill hands that are clenched in fear—release to receive."

Lifting the Veil

"Judgment is the veil that clouds understanding; lift it, and you will see the humanity we all share."

Listening Beyond Labels

"Understanding begins when we stop labelling others and start listening to their untold truths."

Loss is a Lantern

"What feels like loss is often the soul rearranging itself into something more whole."

Manifest Through Meaning

"A goal rooted in ego fades, but a dream seeded in meaning becomes a force of nature."

Mirrors of the Soul

"Every act you judge in another may mirror an untended wound within yourself."

Outgrowing the Old Skin

"To resist change is to worship a version of yourself you've already outgrown."

Ripple of the Heart

"One act of compassion is never small—it echoes. Through a smile, a listening ear, a helping hand, you become a living thread in the fabric of someone's healing."

Roots Beneath the Storm

"Even the fiercest winds cannot uproot the one who draws strength from within. The storm may howl, but your roots—anchored in self-belief—will hold."

Seeing Beyond the Surface

"To judge is to see the cracks in the surface; to understand is to feel the wholeness within."

Speech as a Reflection of the Mind

"Speech is a mirror of the mind—let it reflect clarity, compassion, and truth."

The Alchemy of Trials

"Adversity does not arrive to break you—it arrives to reveal you. Like fire purifies gold, challenges strip away the surface to uncover the brilliance beneath."

The Art of Letting Go

"A clenched fist can hold nothing new. Release your grip on the past, and your hands will be free to receive what is meant for you."

The Art of Receiving

"Manifestation begins not with wanting, but with believing you are already worthy of what you seek."

The Art of Shedding

"Dissolution is not death—it is the art of shedding what no longer fits your becoming."

The Beauty of Imperfection

"The habit of judgment blinds us to the beauty of imperfection, both in others and in ourselves."

The Beauty of Imperfection

"You don't have to be flawless to be significant in someone's story; you just need a heart willing to care and a soul brave enough to show it."

The Beauty of the Journey

"It is not the destination that shapes us, but the road we travel—each step, each stumble, each quiet triumph along the way."

The Climb is the Becoming

"It is not the summit that shapes you, but the climb. Every stumble, every breathless step, every moment you chose not to quit—this is where your soul learns to fly."

The Compass of Joy

"Your joy is not a reward; it is your compass—follow it, and you'll find the life meant for you."

The Cost of Becoming

"Becoming who you are meant to be will cost you who you used to be—pay it gladly."

The Courage to Care

"To make a difference in someone's life, you don't need perfection or grandeur—just the courage to care deeply and the kindness to show it."

The Dance of Faith and Reason

"Wisdom is not choosing between logic and faith—it is knowing when to listen to one and when to trust the other."

The Dance of Knowing

"True wisdom is not the dominance of mind, but the dance of trust and awareness."

The Dance of the Universe

"The stars do not compete in their shining, nor do the rivers envy the sea. Everything flows in harmony—only man resists the rhythm of existence."

The Depth of Listening

"Listening is not just hearing words; it's opening your heart to understand the unspoken emotions and truths within them."

The Depth of True Understanding

"True understanding requires us to pause, listen, and look beyond the surface—into the heart of another's experience."

The Final Lesson

"In the end, no wealth, no title, no possession remains—only the love we gave, the kindness we offered, and the lives we touched."

The Fire That Calls

"Dreams are not mere desires; they are soul-maps—etched into your spirit long before the world told you what was possible. To follow them is not ambition; it is remembrance."

The Flow of Trust

"To flow with the universe is to dance with the unseen, trusting that what is meant cannot miss you."

The Freedom of Letting Go

"To truly be free is not to possess everything, but to release what has anchored you to a past you cannot change, and embrace the open horizon ahead."

The Gentle Power

"The river does not conquer the stone—it wears it down with grace."

The Gentle Power of Love

"Love does not shout to be heard—it whispers where the wounds are, and somehow, that's enough."

The Gentle Strength

"Kindness is not weakness—it is a silent revolution. A soft touch in a hardened world, it breaks walls that words cannot and heals wounds unseen."

The Gift Beneath the Wound

"Some wounds do not vanish—they transform. In their quiet ache lies the strength to rise, the wisdom to guide, and the grace to understand what joy alone could never teach."

The Gift of Presence

"The greatest gift you can offer in a conversation is your presence, for in true listening lies the seed of connection and healing."

The Grace of the Past

"True healing begins the moment we stop trying to erase the past and instead learn to hold it with grace."

The Haven Within

"What we thought was the end was often just love, waiting patiently beneath the ache, asking to be let in."

The Illusion of Time

"Yesterday is a whisper, tomorrow a dream. Only this moment breathes—if you miss it, you miss everything."

The Invisible Light

"Love given freely, without demand or expectation, becomes light in places we may never see. Kindness travels where our footsteps never will."

The Language of the Soul

"The soul doesn't speak in words—it speaks in stillness, in silence, and in the ache we try so hard to hide."

The Light That Bends

"True light does not retreat from shadow; it bends toward the broken, refusing to leave us unseen."

The Light You Are

"You were never meant to chase light—you were born to remember you are it."

The Love We Deserve

"We search for love in a thousand places, not realizing that the most sacred kind is the one we give ourselves when we choose to stay, even in our darkest hour."

The Mirror Within

"You are not what the world sees, but what your soul remembers when everything else is silent. In the stillness, your true self emerges—not as an image, but as an essence."

The Mirror of the Mind

"The world reflects what you believe about yourself. A mind filled with fear sees obstacles, but a heart filled with trust sees possibilities."

The Ocean and the Drop

"A single drop may think itself small, but once it surrenders to the ocean, it becomes infinite. So too, when we dissolve our ego, we become boundless."

The Path to Meaningful Relationships

"The path to meaningful relationships begins with mindful speech; every word you speak shapes the trust, respect, and connection you build."

The Power of Presence

"Manifestation doesn't begin with the future; it begins by meeting yourself fully in the now."

The Prison of the Mind

"No chains are heavier than the ones forged by our own thoughts. Break free, and the whole sky becomes your home."

The Question That Guides

"The most profound journeys begin not with answers, but with a single, honest question: Who am I, when no one is watching, and nothing is expected?"

The Quiet Power of Kindness

"The power to change a life lies not in riches or beauty, but in the simple, quiet moments when you choose to care more than the world expects."

The Root of Connection

"True communication begins where judgment ends and empathy takes root."

The Root of Suffering

"A bird caged all its life fears the open sky. We, too, hold onto our chains, mistaking them for security. True freedom begins when we release what was never ours to hold."

The Sacred Becoming

"You are not chasing a future; you are unfolding into the truth that has always lived within you."

The Sacred Break

"The soul does not break to be destroyed; it breaks to be revealed."

The Sacred Leap

"Between fear and faith lies a sacred space—the moment you leap, not knowing if you will fly, but trusting that your wings will remember how."

The Seed of Greatness

"A mighty tree begins as a seed buried in darkness. Do not fear the trials of today—they are merely preparing you for the heights of tomorrow."

The Silent Teacher

"A tree does not speak, yet it teaches patience. A river does not argue, yet it shows persistence. The sky does not seek attention, yet it holds the entire universe. Wisdom speaks loudest in silence."

The Simplicity of Kindness

"The beauty of language lies not in its complexity, but in its ability to convey kindness, uplift spirits, and build understanding."

The Slow Fade

"Stagnation wears the mask of safety, but its silence drowns the call to become."

The Soul's Timeline

"The soul does not measure time by clocks, but by alignment."

The Strength Within Silence

"True strength is not forged in noise and applause, but in the quiet moments when no one sees your battle—only your soul does, and it chooses to rise again."

The Transformative Power of Gratitude

"Gratitude transforms ordinary conversations into profound connections, infusing words with the power of love."

The Transformative Power of Words

"When you choose words rooted in love and integrity, you don't just transform conversations—you transform lives."

The Unseen Bridges

"The step you fear the most often leads to the path you were meant to walk. Trust that the bridge will appear when you move forward."

The Unshakable Core

"You are not defined by what breaks you, but by the stillness that remains when everything else has fallen away. That is your unshakable core—untouched, eternal."

The Wall and the Bridge

"Judgment is the wall we build to protect our egos, but understanding is the bridge we create to connect our souls."

The Weight of Doubt

"Doubt is not a wall that blocks your path—it is the fog that clouds your vision. Walk forward, and the mist will clear."

The Weight of Negativity

"Negative words are like stones in a river; they obstruct the flow of understanding and drown connection."

The Weight of Unseen Choices

"Not all karma is loud — some lives are shaped by silent decisions the world never witnesses."

The Wellspring Within

"The ancients didn't have more answers—they simply listened more deeply. The same silence that cradled their insight is within us, if only we dare to pause."

The Whisper of the Soul

"Your soul never shouts, but its whisper is louder than the world if you are willing to listen."

Tools for Connection

"Criticism builds walls; curiosity builds bridges. Choose your tools wisely."

Trust in Speech

"To speak with care is to sow seeds of trust; to speak with disregard is to scatter weeds of discord."

Truth Beyond Time

"Life may evolve, but the essence of truth remains unchanged. What guided the hearts of generations before us still pulses beneath our choices—love, humility, and grace."

Unlearning the Cage

"Freedom is not something you attain—it is something you remember once you stop clinging to the bars of your own mind."

Where the Light Enters

"Sometimes, the heart breaks not to destroy us, but to reveal the places where light was always waiting to enter."

Whispers of Becoming

"Your aspirations are whispers from your future self—calling you forward, not to escape the present, but to evolve through it with purpose and grace."

Wholeness in Brokenness

"The beauty of life lies not in perfection, but in the way we accept our broken pieces. Each imperfection is a unique part of the whole, and through acceptance, we become whole in ways we never imagined."

Words as Tools of Creation

"When we focus on solutions instead of problems, our words become tools of creation rather than destruction."

Your Soul is a Compass

"When your actions begin to reflect the wisdom of your soul, the path unfolds without force."

Finding Inner Strength

Empowering the Mind and Spirit

"Strength isn't forged in ease, but in the quiet moments when you refuse to give up. The fiercest power is the one that rises when no one is watching."

- *Shree Shambav*

Abundance of the Mind

"Wealth begins with the belief that abundance is your birthright. Manifesting prosperity isn't about chasing it, it's about aligning with it."

Alchemy of Emotion

"Every emotion is sacred—anger, grief, joy, longing. When held with awareness, even pain becomes gold."

Breaking Free from Self-Imposed Limits

"The barriers you perceive in life are not the walls of the world, but the limits set by beliefs that have yet to be transformed."

Breath of Becoming

"Inhale not just air, but possibility. Exhale not just carbon, but the version of you that no longer fits."

Divine Timing

"Not all delays are denials; some are divine pauses where the soul prepares to receive what the mind cannot yet hold."

Echoes of the Divine

"When you walk with awareness, every moment becomes a message from the universe written in your own footsteps."

Entangled in the Infinite

"In the fabric of existence, all things are entangled, connected beyond time and space. We are not separate from the universe; we are its living, breathing expression. What we think, we become, for our energy is woven into the cosmos."

Healing From Within

"The body listens to the whispers of the mind and heart—manifest your health by nourishing both with love, belief, and alignment."

Healing Through Compassion

"When you approach others with compassion instead of criticism, you invite healing into every conversation."

Hearts That Remember

"You were not born to chase light — you were born to remember you are made of it."

Infinite Shades of Colour

"Judgment narrows the world into black and white; understanding paints it in infinite shades of colour."

Language as Art

"Words are not fleeting sounds; they are the brushstrokes of the soul, painting the canvas of our relationships."

Oneness

"In the dance between the personal mind and the universal cosmos, creation flows effortlessly—when we align our steps with the rhythm of the universe, manifestation becomes our natural expression."

Rebuilding Your Inner World

"Beliefs are not just thoughts; they are the architects of your reality, laying the foundation for every experience you encounter."

Returning to Original Light

"Beneath every limiting belief lies your original light, waiting to be remembered, not created."

Sacred Participation

"The Universe is not a vending machine for desires. It is a dance partner. You must step forward to meet the rhythm."

Sacred Surrender

"Let go not because you've lost hope, but because you've finally trusted the flow that carries stars."

The Blueprint of Dreams

"The journal is a sacred space where thoughts and dreams are crystallised into tangible paths. Write with clarity, for the universe follows the trail you lay with your pen."

The Boulder's Wisdom

"Obstacles are not walls to stop you; they are mountains to elevate your vision."

The Breath Before Becoming

"Between the thought and the thing, there is a breath — in that breath, belief chooses whether you will soar or stumble."

The Breath of Trust

"When you trust the journey, even the detours become sacred."

The Bridge of Belief

"Belief is the bridge between the invisible and the inevitable. Walk it with faith, and the unseen will take form."

The Compass Within

"When the world pulls you in all directions, sit still. The soul speaks in compass points, not noise."

The Compass Within

"Your beliefs are not cages, but maps — if you dare to redraw them, your world redraws itself."

The Compass Within

"External validation fades. But inner alignment never loses direction — it is the compass that never betrays your becoming."

The Compass of Creation

"To realign your beliefs is to recalibrate the compass of your soul — suddenly, every step leads toward a destiny you once thought impossible."

The Cosmic Conversation

"Every thought, every intention, is a whisper in the cosmic dialogue. When we listen closely, the universe speaks to us in ways beyond understanding."

The Currency of Intention

"The universe trades not in words or effort, but in energy. Intention is your wealth; alignment, your investment."

The Dance of Creation

"Karma and manifestation are two rhythms of the same cosmic song — one remembers, the other creates."

The Dance of Creation

"To become the architect of your destiny, you must first align with the flow of the universe. The power lies not in the struggle, but in the surrender to the cosmic rhythm that guides your soul."

The Dance of Thought and Action

"A dream confined to thought is a bird with clipped wings, but when aligned action meets intention, even the impossible takes flight."

The Echoes of Eternity

"Your soul's story is written across lifetimes, but the pen rests in your hands today."

The Fire That Frees

"Sometimes we must burn—not to suffer, but to become light enough to rise."

The Fire Within

"Even when the world turns cold, there remains within you a flame that no storm can extinguish."

The First Act of Power

"The first act of true power is not action, but the courage to believe differently."

The Frequency of Becoming

"You are not a fixed being walking through a static world; you are a wave of energy in constant conversation with the cosmos, shaping and reshaping life with every intention you hold."

The Gatekeeper Within

"Doubt does not block the door to your destiny — it becomes the door. Walk through it, and it opens into faith."

The Grace of Stillness

"When you learn to be still amidst chaos, you stop being tossed by the waves and start becoming the ocean."

The Invisible Foundation

"Strength is often unseen — like roots beneath a great tree, it holds you steady through unseen storms."

The Invisible Loom

"Every thought you cradle, every emotion you nurture, becomes a thread woven into the silent tapestry of your reality."

The Invisible Sculptor

"Your thoughts are the architects, your emotions the builders, and your actions the paint — all vibrating in harmony to create the canvas of your reality."

The Journey to Wholeness

"You are not here to be perfect; you are here to be whole — every crack, every fall, every triumph included."

The Key of Conscious Creation

"Life will write your story if you don't hold the pen — but when intention becomes your ink and belief your paper, the universe has no choice but to read it aloud."

The Language Beyond Words

"Before the universe listens to your words, it first hears the emotions that speak beneath them."

The Language of Silence

"Silence is not emptiness; it is the voice of the soul unburdened by noise, fluent in truth."

The Language of Silence

"Some lessons are not spoken — they are etched in the silent spaces between the heartbeats."

The Library Beyond Time

"The Akashic Records do not predict your future — they illuminate the paths your soul has always known, waiting for you to choose with awareness."

The Light Beneath the Stone

"Beneath every heavy burden you carry, there is hidden light waiting to be set free."

The Magnetic Heart

"When the heart vibrates in harmony with desire, the universe cannot help but respond in kind."

The Mind's Mirror

"As we shift the mirror of our consciousness, the universe reflects the truth of our thoughts, revealing the boundless possibilities of creation."

The Mirror Beyond Glass

"The world you walk through is only the reflection of the world you carry within."

The Mirror of Adversity

"Adversity is not your enemy; it is the mirror in which your truest self is revealed."

The Mirror of All Existence

"Every thought, intention, and choice is etched into the infinite — the Akashic Records do not forget, they simply wait for you to remember."

The Mirror of Cause

"Karma is not fate's punishment, but the echo of your own intentions returning home."

The Mirror of Existence

"The universe is not a distant force beyond your reach; it is the mirror of your inner world, faithfully reflecting the story you choose to tell yourself."

The Mirror of Infinity

"Your mind is not a closed chamber but an open mirror — reflecting and shaping the infinite intelligence that surrounds you."

The Mirror of Manifestation

"The world you see is not outside you—it is the echo of the beliefs you refuse to examine."

The Mirror of Self-Love

"The world around you only echoes the truth you dare to whisper within; when you choose to love yourself deeply, the universe rushes to mirror that love back to you."

The Mirror of the Mind

"The universe is not responding to your words, but to the vibration behind them — your true intentions."

The Path Carved by Faith

"Each scar upon your heart is not a wound, but a map leading you back to your invincible spirit."

The Patience of Becoming

"Growth does not scream; it whispers, waiting patiently for the soul to awaken and remember its own vastness."

The Power of Belief in Manifestation

"The world around you is the echo of your deepest beliefs. Change those beliefs, and you change the world you create."

The Power of Co-Creation

"You are not a passive observer of life's unfolding; you are a creator, co-designing every moment with the universe's infinite intelligence."

The Power of Connection

"When you align your energy with the intention of love, relationships no longer feel like a chase; they become a natural flow, effortlessly drawn toward you."

The Power of Intentional Speech

"Every word you speak is a choice: to add light or cast shadow, to build bridges or raise walls. Speak with intention, for your words shape the world you share."

The Power of Words

"The words we speak are the brushstrokes painting the canvas of our reality. Speak with intention, for your thoughts manifest into form with every syllable you utter."

The Power of the Observer

"As we observe, we become the creators. Our consciousness doesn't merely witness the world; it shapes it. In the quantum realm, the act of observing bends the fabric of reality, empowering us to manifest our deepest desires."

The Pulse of Creation

"Emotion is the silent architect that gives form to thought — without its rhythm, even the clearest intention remains unbuilt."

The Pulse of Existence

"The universe does not speak in words — it hums in frequencies. To understand its language, one must first learn to listen, not with ears, but with awareness."

The Pulse of Purpose

"When you align with your soul's purpose, even silence becomes music, and every step becomes a prayer."

The Quantum Dance of Creation

"The universe doesn't simply exist outside of us; it responds to our consciousness. In the quantum field, thought and matter are not separate but intertwined, constantly communicating in a dance of creation."

The Quiet Alchemy

"Transformation is not loud; it begins quietly, when a single limiting belief crumbles and light rushes in to take its place."

The Sacred Pause

"Between intention and action lies a stillness — not of waiting, but of listening. That space is where the soul whispers its clearest truth."

The Sacred in the Ordinary

"Enlightenment is not found in escape, but in presence—in washing a dish as if it were the face of the Divine."

The Sculptor

"Beliefs sculpt the invisible before it becomes visible; reality is only the statue unveiled by the unseen hand."

The Sculptor's Choice

"Every action plants a seed, but it is conscious manifestation that decides the shape of the harvest."

The Seed Within

"Within every belief lies a seed — if nourished by fear, it grows into walls; if nourished by trust, it grows into wings."

The Seed of Reality

"Every thought is a seed, planted in the soil of the universe. Nurtured by emotion, it grows into the reality you call your life."

The Shadow's Blessing

"What you hide in shame is not your flaw, but the part of you waiting to be loved into wholeness."

The Silence of Creation

"In the stillness of the mind, we find the fertile soil where our desires take root. It is through silence that the universe begins to speak back to us."

The Silent Architect

"Every thought you repeat, every emotion you nurture, quietly lays the bricks of the life you call your own."

The Silent Architect

"Manifestation is not magic — it is the silent architecture of belief, emotion, and unwavering intent constructing your future, moment by moment."

The Seed of Reality

"Every thought you nurture is a seed planted in the garden of existence; belief waters it, emotion nourishes it, and action brings it into bloom."

The Silent Architect

"Your destiny is not written in stone, but in vibration — the Akashic Records whisper the design, and your heart completes the blueprint."

The Silent Architect

"Your unseen beliefs draft the blueprint of your reality, long before your hands ever shape it."

The Silent Revolution

"The greatest revolutions are not fought in the world, but in the quiet rebellion against the beliefs that once held us small."

The Song of Endurance

"Those who endure silently sing the most sacred songs — the music only the soul can hear."

The Spark of Encouragement

"A single word of encouragement can ignite a fire of hope; a single word of criticism can extinguish a dream. Choose wisely."

The Stillness Between Steps

"True transformation does not occur in motion, but in the pause between thoughts where the soul remembers itself."

The Stone and the Spirit

"The rock teaches not through words, but through presence — unyielding, silent, eternal."

The Strength of Empathy

"Replacing judgment with empathy is not weakness; it's the strength to choose connection over division."

The Strength of Surrender

"True resilience is not resistance but surrender — surrendering to the wisdom that every fall is part of the dance."

The Symphony of Co-Creation

"Creation is not an act of will, but of resonance — when your soul vibrates in harmony with the cosmos, the universe sings through you."

The Weaver's Whisper

"Your reality is not written by chance but woven by the unseen threads of your beliefs and feelings."

The Weight of Unspoken Truths

"What we do not say becomes the weight we silently carry—until honesty sets it down and love picks it up."

Trust the Blueprint

"The universe has already drafted your soul's blueprint. Your task is not to force your way, but to trust the path that unfolds, knowing that every step is divinely guided."

Vibration is Destiny

"Your future doesn't unfold from plans—it blossoms from your frequency."

When Silence Speaks

"True alignment begins in stillness — when the noise of the self dissolves, the universe whispers back in the language of knowing."

Whispers of Worthiness

"The world will mirror your belief in yourself. Whisper 'I am enough' into your being until it becomes the loudest truth you know."

Whispers of the Inner Child

"Before you manifest the life you want, return to the child within who once imagined without fear."

Wounds as Portals

"Pain is not a punishment but a portal. Every wound, when honored, becomes a doorway to deeper light."

Gratitude and Mindfulness

Finding Joy in the Present

"In the quiet stillness of the present moment, we find the vast expanse of eternity. Mindfulness is the art of stepping into the now, where joy is not a destination, but a way of being."

- Shree Shambav

A Full Cup of Nothingness

"When the cup of life is too full, even a drop overflows. Emptiness, embraced, becomes the canvas for abundance."

A Path Uncluttered

"Walking an uncluttered path allows the soul to breathe. Simplicity paves the way for a life of meaning and grace."

Alchemy of Awareness

"Awareness turns reaction into reflection, and karma into a ladder rather than a loop."

Alchemy of the Heart

"Every wound you heal with love becomes a doorway to your higher self."

Break the Loop, Begin the Light

"The loops of karma dissolve the moment you respond with awareness instead of habit."

Bridge of Trust

"Fear builds walls; trust builds bridges to your dreams."

Cherishing Blind Trust

"Blind trust is a rare gift; cherish it, honour it, and never let it fall into the shadows of regret."

Divine Timing

"The universe doesn't work by your deadlines; it responds to your readiness."

Embrace the Unknown

"Faith is not the absence of fear, but the willingness to move with it toward light."

Embracing Life's Ebb and Flow

"To breathe mindfully is to embrace life's ebb and flow, to find a balance in the midst of turbulence, and to awaken to the profound truth that peace is not found in the absence of storms but in the quiet strength to weather them."

Experiences Over Excess

"Experiences etch memories on the soul; material possessions merely gather dust in forgotten corners."

Frequency of Truth

"Your vibration doesn't lie; it sings the story your soul has long carried in silence."

From Complaints to Bridges

"Complaints are the rocks in our path, but solutions are the bridges we build to cross them. Change your perspective, and every obstacle becomes an opportunity for growth."

Fuel of the Heart

"Self-love is not a luxury on the journey of manifestation — it is the fuel."

Growth Over Gold

"Personal growth outshines gold, for it enriches your soul and illuminates the path to meaning."

Growth through Adversity

"Adversity is the soil in which resilience grows. Without the storms, there would be no roots to hold you steady. Embrace challenges as the nurturing force of your growth."

Harmony in Gratitude and Mindfulness

"Gratitude and mindfulness are twin flames of peace. Together, they illuminate the beauty of the present and remind us that joy is not something to chase—it is something to embrace."

Letting Go as Liberation

"Manifestation begins not when you grasp tighter, but when your palms open to receive."

Liberation Through Selflessness

"To serve without expectation, to give without attachment, is to touch the infinite. In that moment, you are no longer a seeker—you are free."

Light Beneath the Stone

"Your heaviest burdens often guard the brightest revelations — waiting to be seen with inner eyes."

Living as the Prayer

"Don't just ask the universe for a blessing — become the kind of person who embodies the answer."

Redefining Wealth

"True wealth lies not in what you own, but in the richness of your experiences, the depth of your relationships, and the growth of your inner self."

Resilience in Empowerment

"Empowerment begins in the mind and flows into the spirit. When you believe in your own resilience, no challenge can shatter the foundation of your will."

Roots Before Wings

"Before your dreams can fly, they must first take root in the soil of self-awareness and surrender."

Roots of Joy

"Happiness grows not in having more, but in needing less. Contentment is the soil where joy takes root."

Sacred Detours

"What feels like delay is often divine choreography — guiding you where your soul is truly meant to bloom."

Sacred Discontent

"The ache in your soul isn't a punishment — it's the pull of your potential begging you to rise."

Sacred Disruption

"When the soul is ready to grow, it often chooses discomfort as a teacher."

Simplicity in Fulfilment

"When we find joy in simplicity, we realise that contentment is the richest form of wealth, while endless desire is the deepest poverty."

Stillness Has Wings

"True transformation doesn't roar — it arrives on silent wings, in moments of still, surrendered clarity."

Success Has a Price

"A child may climb the highest mountains of success, but if they forget the hands that once lifted them, their victory will echo with emptiness."

The Anchor of Attachment

"Your life is like a boat tethered by the chains of material wealth; freedom comes when you release the chains and sail into the open sea of life's true potential."

The Art of Letting Go

"Let go of the need to control, and watch your life align with grace."

The Art of Letting Go

"Letting go is not losing; it is gaining freedom. To release what no longer serves is to make space for what does."

The Art of Letting Go

"To hold on too tightly is to deny the flow of life. Love does not ask us to cling; it asks us to trust that what is real never truly leaves."

The Art of Presence

"Mindfulness is the art of being fully alive in the now. It turns ordinary moments into extraordinary blessings and teaches the heart to find joy in simplicity."

The Art of Remembering

"Manifestation is not about creating something new, but about remembering who you truly are."

The Becoming

"Manifestation is not about forcing outcomes but becoming the version of you who naturally receives them."

The Bridge of Gratitude

"Gratitude is the bridge between what you have and the joy you seek. When you pause to cherish the present, you realise life's smallest moments hold the greatest treasures."

The Burden of Desire

"To constantly want is to live in scarcity, but contentment is the key that unlocks a life of abundance."

The Chains of Materialism

"Material possessions promise comfort but often deliver chains. Liberation comes from placing value on what feeds the soul, not the ego."

The Compass of Purpose

"Purpose is the compass that guides us through the noise. When life is aligned, even the mundane becomes sacred."

The Dance of Cause and Choice

"Life moves between karma and free will — one reveals your patterns, the other your power."

The Dance of Decisions

"Every choice is a step in the dance of life. Choose only those that lead you toward harmony and purpose."

The Echo of Every Act

"Every small act holds the weight of eternity — a kindness planted now may blossom in a lifetime unseen."

The Echo of Intention

"What you whisper in the silence of your heart becomes the echo that shapes your destiny."

The Echo of Time

"Time whispers to those who listen: it is not how much you do, but how deeply you live, that creates meaning."

The Echo of the Past

"The past never truly leaves us. It lingers in the voices we remember, the hands we once held, and the roads we never thought we would walk again."

The Essence of Understanding

"True understanding isn't just about hearing words; it's about feeling the unspoken, sensing the heart behind the voice, and embracing the complexity of the human experience."

The Eternal Chase

"The pursuit of material wealth is a race with no finish line, while the pursuit of wisdom and connection leads to a life well-lived."

The Fog of Ignorance

"Ignorance is not absence—it is presence disguised. It wraps itself in comfort, fear, and pride, and says, 'This is who I am.' To awaken, we must question the voice that claims to protect us by keeping us small."

The Freedom of Surrender

"The moment we stop fighting the current, we feel the river carry us. Surrender is not defeat—it is trust. When we embrace truth, resistance melts, and the soul remembers how to fly."

The Friend Within

"Conquer your mind, and it will guide you to peace; let it rule you, and it will lead you into chaos."

The Garden of Fulfillment

"A fulfilling life is like a thriving garden; it blossoms when you nurture personal growth and cultivate meaningful relationships."

The Gift of Enough

"Enough is not measured by how much we have, but by how much we appreciate. The greatest wealth is contentment."

The Gift of Relationships

"Relationships are life's greatest treasures, offering a connection that no material possession can replicate."

The Gift of Trust

"When someone places their blind trust in you, let your actions prove their faith was not misplaced but deeply earned."

The Gratitude Code

"Gratitude is the frequency that tells the universe, 'I am ready to receive more.'"

The Illusion of Ownership

"You do not own the earth, the sky, or even the breath in your lungs—everything is borrowed for a time. To give freely is to honor the truth that nothing truly belongs to us."

The Illusion of Ownership

"You do not possess material things—they possess you, anchoring your soul and blinding you to the joy of simplicity."

The Inner Garden

"Your mind is a garden; tend it well. Weed out distractions, water it with stillness, and watch peace bloom."

The Journey Within

"Your highest manifestation isn't something you get — it's someone you become on the way."

The Language of Light

"Gratitude is how the soul speaks when words are too small for the miracle of being."

The Language of the Soul

"Gratitude is the soul's silent prayer, a bridge between what we have and the joy we seek."

The Legacy of Love

"In the end, the legacy of a life well-lived is not in possessions left behind, but in the love and experiences shared along the way."

The Light Within Shadows

"Even the longest night cannot prevent the dawn. Even in sorrow, there is a light within you—waiting, patient, ready to rise."

The Measure of Wealth

"A man is not measured by the weight of his gold, but by the weight his kindness carries in the hearts of others."

The Mirror We Avoid

"Truth does not punish—it reflects. But we fear the mirror, for it shows us what we must release. Resistance is not against life—it is against seeing ourselves clearly."

The Mirror of Life

"What we keep reflects who we are. Decluttering is not just cleaning; it is rediscovering the person we long to be."

The Mirror of Life

"What you attract is not what you want, but what you believe you deserve."

The Open Hand

"Happiness is like an open hand; when you stop clutching at possessions, you are free to hold, release, and receive with grace."

The Paradox of Giving

"The more love, kindness, and wisdom you give, the more you become filled with them. In giving, you do not lose—you expand."

The Peace of Simplicity

"Simplicity is the art of living lightly, so that the soul can rest deeply. In its embrace, we find our truest peace."

The Power of Perspective

"Your thoughts shape the world you see. When you change your perspective, you change your reality—transforming obstacles into opportunities and struggles into strengths."

The Power of Presence

"You don't need to chase alignment; you need only return to the now—where all power resides."

The Power of Release

"In letting go of what weighs you down, you find a lightness that allows you to rise into your most authentic self."

The Quiet Truth of Simplicity

"Peace resides not in abundance but in simplicity—the quiet joy of being present and enough."

The Rhythm of Life

"In the rhythm of your breath, you discover the rhythm of your life—a dance of inhaling hope and exhaling fear, of embracing the present and releasing the past, of finding harmony within the very essence of your being."

The Sacred Bond of Trust

"To be trusted without question is a sacred bond—guard it with integrity, for it reflects the strength of your character."

The Sanctuary of the Present

"Each mindful breath is an invitation to return to yourself, to shed the weight of past regrets and future worries, and to dwell in the sanctuary of the present moment, where true healing begins."

The Seeds of Fate

"A simple act of kindness is like a seed carried by the wind. It may take root in places unseen, growing into something far greater than the one who planted it could ever imagine."

The Shore of Contentment

"Material wealth is like a shore that feels safe, yet it is the open sea of relationships and self-discovery where true fulfillment resides."

The Silence Between Breaths

"In the stillness between your thoughts lies the voice of the universe — whispering not what you want, but who you truly are."

The Silence of the Heart

"In the stillness of the heart, we hear the loudest truths. Silence is not emptiness; it is fullness waiting to be felt."

The Silent Messenger

"Your energy introduces your desires long before your words ever do."

The Soul's Whisper

"The soul doesn't scream; it whispers — and those whispers shape your destiny."

The Strength of Silence

"Sometimes, silence speaks louder than words. In moments of stillness, the heart listens, the mind reflects, and the soul finds clarity."

The Tide of Fate

"One may sail with a map in hand, but the sea will always have its course. Destiny does not ask where you wish to go—it carries you where you belong."

The True Wealth of Contentment

"To live in constant want is to dwell in poverty, for true richness comes from contentment, not possessions."

The Truth of Recognition

"To be recognised not for what you have become, but for who you were before the world shaped you, is a rare and humbling gift."

The Unfinished Story

"Grief is not the end of love's story; it is the chapter where we learn to love differently—without presence, but never without feeling."

The Unshakable Flame

"True strength is born in moments of doubt and fear. It is the unshakable flame within that refuses to be extinguished, even when the world feels heavy on your shoulders."

The Waiting Game

"You are not waiting for the universe — the universe is waiting for you to believe."

The Wealth Within

"True success is not measured by what you accumulate, but by the peace and wisdom you cultivate within."

The Wealth of Contentment

"True wealth lies not in what we possess, but in the peace we feel when we are content with what we have."

The Wealth of an Open Hand

"That which we cling to imprisons us, but that which we give away sets us free. True wealth is not measured by what we accumulate, but by what we share."

The Weight of Simplicity

"Simplicity is not the absence of possessions but the presence of clarity. When we remove the unnecessary, we reveal the essence of our purpose."

The Weight of Unspoken Words

"A heart filled with unspoken truths is like a river bound by ice—silent on the surface, but turbulent underneath. Speak with courage, for words left unsaid become burdens too heavy to carry."

Wholeness is the Way

"You don't manifest from what you lack, but from the part of you that remembers it was never broken."

Words as Seeds

"Every word you speak plants a seed. Whether it grows into a flower of understanding or a weed of discord is up to you. Choose your words as carefully as you would choose the seeds for a garden."

Inspiration and Motivation

Fuelling the Soul

"Inspiration is the spark that awakens the dormant fire within. It does not push us forward; it illuminates the path, reminding us that the journey is just as vital as the destination."

- *Shree Shambav*

Ashes into Light

"True transformation often begins with loss—the letting go of what we once clung to. From the ashes of old identities, a brighter, truer light emerges."

Balancing Worlds

"True strength lies not in choosing between responsibilities but in carrying the weight of both. It is in the balance between ambition and duty that we discover our purpose."

Beyond the Words"

Connection is not built through perfect conversations, but through shared silences, unspoken understanding, and the courage to stay when it's easier to run."

Building Beyond Bricks

"A business built with integrity isn't just a structure of brick and stone—it's a sanctuary of hope, a foundation for futures, and a testament to the power of shared dreams."

Changing the Narrative

"It's never too late to change the narrative of your life and find peace within your heart."

Colour Beyond the Spectrum

"Existence isn't painted in black and white—it is a canvas of unseen hues. Between joy and sorrow, strength and surrender, lies the sacred spectrum of being."

Courage in the Present

"In the face of fleeting time, we find the courage to live fully, knowing that each breath is both a beginning and an end."

Craving Light in Darkness

"Even in the darkest moments, the soul craves the light of purpose and meaning."

Echoes of Grief

"Grief is an unspoken echo, a silent thread woven through the fabric of our souls, reminding us that love and loss are inseparable parts of life's tapestry."

Echoes of the Eternal

"Within every longing is a call to return—not to a place, but to presence. The Divine is not far away; it is the timeless now echoing in your heartbeat."

Embracing the Flow of Life

"When you let go of the need to control every step, life flows through you with ease, and your manifestations unfold effortlessly."

Eternal Bond

"A mother's love is a symphony of kindness, resonating through every heartbeat and shaping the soul with her gentle touch."

Finding Courage in Reflection

"In the quiet of reflection, we often find the courage to face our deepest fears."

Freedom Through Forgiveness

"Forgiveness is the key to freeing ourselves from the chains of past mistakes."

Key to Inner Peace

"In the quiet depths of introspection, we meet the parts of ourselves we often hide, finding that self-discovery is the key to inner peace and boundless growth."

Living as a Lifelong Creator

"Manifestation is not a single act but the art of living consciously every day, knowing that every thought, every emotion, and every action shapes your reality."

Love Beyond Life

"Even in the face of death, love remains the most powerful force of all. True love transcends the boundaries of life and death."

Nature's Whisper

"In the gentle rustle of leaves and the soft embrace of sunlight, nature whispers secrets of serenity, reminding us that beauty resides not just in grand vistas, but in the simple, quiet moments of existence."

On Everyday Decisions

"To simplify a decision is to quiet the noise of 'more' and listen to the whisper of 'essential.'"

On Inner Clarity

"Decluttering your outer world is a mere rehearsal; the true performance lies in decluttering your mind and soul."

On Life's True Riches

"Minimalism is not the absence of possessions; it is the presence of clarity and abundance in what truly matters."

On Material Possessions

"Possessions can serve or enslave; the minimalist asks, 'Does this serve my soul?'"

On Meaningful Relationships

"True connection is not built on the weight of expectation but on the lightness of acceptance and authenticity."

On the Path to Peace

"Peace is not found in more—it is unearthed in the quiet, intentional spaces where simplicity thrives."

Presence as a Portal

"To receive more from life, become more present to it."

Richness in Simplicity

"It's in the simplest of moments—a warm cup, a soft laugh, a gentle breeze—that we uncover the richness of life."

Sacred Mirrors

"In every relationship, we meet not just the other—but ourselves. Love reveals the parts we hide, heals the wounds we deny, and invites us to grow through the reflection of another's soul."

Solace Under the Moon

"Under the quiet gaze of the moon, our hearts find solace and our souls dance with the secrets of the night sky."

Spaces Between

"In the dance of love, we embrace the paradox of intimacy and distance, discovering that true connection often flourishes in the spaces between us."

Stars as Storytellers

"In the silence of night, the stars become our storytellers, guiding us through dreams and mysteries only the darkness dares reveal."

Strength in Sorrow

"In sorrow's shadow, we find depth and resilience, learning that even the heaviest burdens transform us, revealing new strength and compassion."

The Art of Letting Go

"Freedom begins the moment you release what no longer serves your heart, your purpose, or your peace."

The Art of Rising

"We are not defined by our struggles, but by the grace with which we rise from them—each scar a mark of wisdom, each tear a testament to resilience."

The Art of Seeing

"Two souls may stand before the same horizon—one sees a sunset, the other a dawn. Perception shapes destiny."

The Balance of Life

"Simplicity is not about depriving yourself but about aligning with what nourishes and sustains your deepest self."

The Beauty of the Shadow

"Do not fear your shadow—it is proof that the light exists behind you. Every sorrow you carry is a contour of the life you've dared to live."

The Breath Between Stars

"Every silence between your thoughts, every pause between your breaths, is where the Divine whispers. The universe does not shout—it waits patiently in your stillness."

The Chrysalis Within

"Change does not come to break you; it comes to awaken the wings folded within you. The pain you feel is not the end—it is the hush before you fly."

The Dance of Choice

"Life is a series of crossroads, and wisdom is the map that simplifies the journey toward your truth."

The Dance of Life

"True strength is not found in how fiercely we fight the winds of life, but in how gently we learn to dance with them."

The Dance of Love

"Love is a delicate dance, weaving joy and longing into a tapestry of emotions, where every step reveals the beauty of vulnerability and connection."

The Discipline of Enough

"When you learn to say, 'This is enough,' you discover that enough is a state of grace, not a limitation."

The Echoes of Growth

"True success is not in how far you go, but in how deeply you remain connected to where you began."

The Essence of Peace

"True peace resides not in the absence of noise, but in the presence of mindfulness, where every breath is a reminder of the beauty found in the now."

The Eternal Flame

"Fear of death dims the flame of life, but to love unconditionally is to light a fire that transcends the boundaries of time and existence."

The Eternal Within

"Your essence is not bound by time or form. It is a silent force, a truth that lies beneath the surface, waiting to be remembered."

The Fleeting Nature of Time

"Time slips through our grasp, like sand between fingers, teaching us to cherish each moment before it fades."

The Foundation of Dreams

"True success isn't built on ambition alone—it rises from the solid foundation of hard work, sacrifice, and the unshakable belief in something greater than yourself."

The Gentle Art of Letting Go

"Balance is not about holding everything together—it's about knowing what to hold and what to release. In letting go of control, we make room for grace."

The Gentle Strength of Minimalism

"Minimalism is not about scarcity; it is about choosing what adds strength and beauty to your life's tapestry."

The Illusion of the World

"The world is but a fleeting shadow, shifting and disappearing with the passage of time. What we chase is not the truth, but an illusion that slips through our fingers."

The Inner Journey

"The journey within leads us to the hidden landscapes of our soul, where every truth we uncover brings us closer to who we truly are."

The Inner Path

"The greatest discovery is not in finding a new place, but in realising that the path to peace is already within."

The Journey to Inner Peace

"The path to inner peace begins when we stop seeking perfection and start embracing authenticity."

The Language of Silence

"In silence, the heart learns to hear what words cannot express."

The Language of the Heart

"Simplicity is the voice of the heart, speaking in tones of love, authenticity, and compassion."

The Legacy of Touching Hearts

"The most profound legacy is not carved in stone but in the hearts of those we touch."

The Light That Burns for Others

"Some souls are like lamps—they burn quietly, giving light to others, never seeking recognition, only hoping that their warmth will be enough to guide the way."

The Light That Needs No Sun

"There is a light within you untouched by sorrow, unchanged by time. Even in your darkest moments, it flickers—quiet, patient, eternal—waiting for you to remember it."

The Light Within

"You don't need to chase the sun — you need to become the light."

The Magnetic Law

"What you radiate, you attract — not by chance, but by law."

The Master and the Student

"A master and a student walk the same path, yet one seeks to learn while the other already knows. The difference is not in the road but in the heart."

The Measure of a Life

"A life's worth is not in what it possesses, but in what it gives, transforms, and leaves behind—just as a simple shawl can become warmth, shelter, and light in different hands."

The Mirror Called Challenge

"Every challenge is not a block, but a mirror — asking if you are aligned with your truth."

The Mirror of Choice

"Life is a mirror, reflecting not who we are, but who we choose to be."

The Path of Self-Discovery

"To know yourself is to return to the source. In shedding the layers of illusion, you come to realise the divine within you has always been there."

The Power of Acceptance

"Your inner peace is not found in perfection, but in acceptance of imperfection."

The Power of Emptiness

"Emptiness is not the absence of being; it is the pure potential of all that exists. In the stillness, the soul finds its true nature."

The Power of Focus

"In a world overflowing with distractions, simplicity is the courage to hold fast to what anchors your soul."

The Power of Gratitude in Creation

"Gratitude is the soul's acknowledgement that the universe is always conspiring in your favour — and when you thank it, you align with its abundant flow."

The Price of Understanding

"Wisdom does not come with age, but with the pain of realizing how blind we were to the hands that built us."

The Quiet Voice of Truth

"Wisdom is not accumulated knowledge; it is the ability to hear the quiet voice of truth amidst the noise of the world."

The Reflection We Deny

"The face we turn away from in shame is often the one that shaped us with love—unseen, unthanked, but never unfelt."

The River's Wisdom

"The river does not resist the bend; it flows with grace, trusting the unseen path. So must we flow with life, not because we know where it leads, but because we trust what we're becoming."

The Roots of Dreams

"Dreams are like trees; their branches reach for the sky, but their strength lies in the unseen roots nurtured by love and resilience."

The Sacred Rhythm

"As the seasons unfurl their tales—each bloom, each frost—a sacred rhythm unfolds, inviting us to dance in harmony with the world, where every cycle reflects the profound interconnectedness of life."

The Sacred Stillness

"Stillness is not the absence of action, but the fullness of alignment."

The Seed of Greatness

"Every moment of despair holds within it the seed of opportunity, but only those who dare to nurture it will see it bloom."

The Seeds of Ambition

"Dreams, like seeds, grow in the soil of effort. Nurture them with patience, water them with belief, and they will one day rise to shade an entire generation."

The Silent Sacrifice

"A parent's love is often invisible—stitched into the nights they stayed awake for you, the dreams they sacrificed, and the wounds they never spoke of."

The Sky Within

"Meditation is the art of discovering the eternal within the transient, the unshakable sky beyond life's fleeting clouds."

The Soul's Liberation

"Every item you release, every thought you simplify, is a step toward the liberation of your spirit."

The Still Point Within

"Peace is not found by escaping the storm but by discovering the stillness that exists within it. When you stop resisting life's chaos, you realise that calm was never outside—it was always within."

The Symphony of Existence

"To truly live is to embrace the beauty of every fleeting moment, for in the dance of life and death lies the symphony of the soul's awakening."

The Threads of Love

"Love is not always spoken—it is stitched into the fabric of life, woven through silent gestures, unwavering patience, and the warmth that shields us when we are too young to understand."

The Timeless Measure

"True maturity is not measured by years or achievements, but by the courage to turn inward and embrace the timeless essence of your being."

The True Measure of Legacy

"Our legacy isn't the things we acquire, but the love, wisdom, and inspiration we leave behind."

The Unseen Sacrifice

"A father's love is not measured in words or wealth, but in the quiet sacrifices no one sees—the nights spent worrying, the days spent building, and the years spent giving without asking."

The Wealth of Perspective

"Some count riches in gold, others in wisdom—one fades with time, the other lasts for eternity."

The Weight of Gratitude

"The burden of love is never heavy for the giver, but it can be crushing for the receiver who forgets its worth."

The Weight of Sacrifice

"Behind every triumph is an unseen thread of sacrifices, woven by those who dreamed of your ascent long before you did."

The Weight of Unspoken Words

"Regret is the heaviest burden, for it carries the words we never said and the love we realised too late."

The Weight of a Good Name

"A reputation is like the first stone of a foundation; if it's laid with care, it can carry the weight of empires. If neglected, even the strongest walls will crumble."

The Wisdom of Less

"In stripping away the excess, we find the core of wisdom—the light of truth that has always been within."

Threads of the Infinite

"What you call coincidence, the soul knows as connection. The Divine weaves its will in the unseen—through people, moments, and the gentle pull of intuition."

Threads of the Unseen

"True love is not loud or demanding—it is the quiet presence that holds you when the world forgets. It is not found in perfect moments, but in imperfect hearts that choose each other, again and again."

Tuning into the Future

"The future is not a place you go — it is a frequency you align with."

Whispers Between Breaths

"In the quiet between two breaths, the soul speaks. To hear it, you must slow down, soften your gaze, and surrender to the sacred now."

Wisdom in Stillness

"In the stillness of the moment, we uncover the profound wisdom hidden within silence, where the world slows down and our hearts can truly listen."

Writing the Story of Your Life

"Let your life be the story you've always wanted to tell, not the chapter left unwritten."

Nature Symphony

Odes to the Earth

"The earth sings in whispers and roars, a melody composed by the winds, rivers, and trees. In its symphony, we find not only the rhythm of life, but the heartbeat of all existence."

- *Shree Shambav*

A Candle's Light

"The light of one candle does not dim by lighting another. The universe is vast—another's success does not diminish your own path."

Becoming the Ocean

"Like a river merging with the ocean, the individual self dissolves into universal consciousness, only to find it was the ocean all along."

Beneath the Banyan

"Stillness beneath an ancient tree can awaken more truth than a thousand pages of scripture — if the heart is ready to listen."

Breath of the Infinite

"Each breath you take is a thread — weaving your soul back into the eternal fabric of the stars."

Drink from the Well Within

"If you thirst for love, become love. If you long for peace, embody peace. The world reflects the water you carry within."

Flow Over Force

"You do not push the river; you learn to flow with it— manifestation begins when effort bows to alignment."

Guiding Light

"In the quiet strength of my mother, I find the divine—her compassion flowing like a river, her love a beacon guiding me home."

Letting the Flame Burn

"You are not lost—you're just standing in the fire that forges who you truly are."

Ocean of Emotion

"The tears in a mother's eyes have the power to make the sea roar, her pain echoing through the depths of the universe."

Roots and Wings

"You are not betraying your roots by growing wings—they were always meant to meet the sky."

Sacred Seeds of Thought

"Each thought you plant in the garden of your mind is a seed — the universe does not question it, only nurtures it into being."

Seeds Beyond Time

"Karma is not a punishment but a seed — planted in thought, watered by action, and harvested in awareness."

Still Waters Create Depth

"In the quiet mind, the soul finds space to speak — and the Universe finds room to respond."

The Art of Inner Weather

"You are the sky, not the storm — and once you realise this, even your darkest clouds begin to shine with light."

The Cage of Hesitation

"A bird born in a cage believes flying is dangerous. Break free from the bars of doubt, and you will remember that the sky was always yours."

The Dance of Time

"Clocks measure time, but only presence measures life. Every moment ignored is a breath unlived."

The Echo of Trust

"The universe responds to your faith in it. When you step forward with trust, the ground beneath you rises to meet your feet."

The Eternal Battle

"The fiercest battles are fought in silence—against the enemies of our own mind. Victory is not in defeating them once, but in rising daily with love, wisdom, and resolve."

The Eternal Fire

"Doubt is the wind that flickers the flame, but faith is the ember that never dies. Even in darkness, trust that the fire still burns within you."

The Eternal Flame

"The light you seek in the stars is the same light that glows within your soul—both are fragments of the eternal flame."

The Fire That Frees

"The fire that undoes you is the same fire that frees you—burn gently, burn true."

The Fire and the Ashes

"You are not just the fire, but the ashes, too. Not just the rising, but the falling. You are every version of yourself that has ever existed."

The Garden Within

"You cannot plant bitterness and expect joy to bloom. Your inner soil determines the fragrance of your outer life."

The Garden of Perception

"Beliefs are the soil where your reality takes root — tend them, and the life you long for begins to bloom."

The Garden of Trust

"Life blossoms not when we control the seasons, but when we trust the seed, the soil, and the unseen sun."

The Language of Compassion

"Compassion is the language of the cosmos, spoken in silence and understood by the heart."

The Language of Stars

"Manifestation is not commanding the universe; it is learning the language of stars — the silent tongue of trust, gratitude, and vision."

The Light Within the Fog

"Clarity isn't the absence of chaos but the courage to see through it—like sunlight breaking through fog, it illuminates not just the path ahead but the strength within."

The Light Within the Storm

"Do not fear the storm—it does not come to break you, but to clear the path ahead. Every lightning strike reveals the way forward."

The Ocean Remembers

"You are not a drop lost in the sea; you are the ocean forgetting itself for a breath, only to remember with a smile."

The Ocean and the Drop

"A single drop resists the ocean out of fear, not knowing that surrender will return it to its infinite self."

The Ocean and the Drop

"You are not a single drop lost in the sea; you are the entire ocean, longing to remember itself. The vastness you seek is not outside of you—it is within, waiting to be found."

The River Remembers

"Even when the path twists and turns, the river never forgets its direction—it flows home without needing a map."

The River and the Rock

"The river does not conquer the rock by force but by patience. Wisdom flows the same way—quiet, persistent, unstoppable."

The River and the Sky

"Some people love like rivers—constantly flowing, touching lives before moving on. Others love like the sky—ever-present, even when unseen. Both are love, both are eternal."

The River of Generosity

"A river that hoards its water becomes a stagnant swamp, but a river that flows nourishes all in its path. A generous heart, like a flowing river, is never empty."

The River's Lesson

"A river never mourns the mountains it leaves behind. It flows forward, carrying their essence within its currents. So too must we carry love, not loss, as we journey ahead."

The River's Wisdom

"A river does not mourn the stones it once struck—it simply flows forward. Learn from the past, but do not let it keep you from moving ahead."

The River's Wisdom

"A river does not question the path before it—it flows, knowing the ocean awaits. Trust the current of your life."

The Roots of Resilience

"True strength lies not in what stands tall and visible but in the unseen roots that weather storms, drawing from the quiet depths of perseverance and grace."

The Seed of Becoming

"A seed does not fear the darkness of the soil, for it knows that growth begins in the unseen. Trust your journey, even when you cannot yet see the light."

The Seed's Secret

"You were not made to stay. Even the seed must shatter to greet the sky."

The Sound of Stillness

"Stillness is not the absence of movement, but the presence of awareness so deep that even silence speaks."

The Stillness of Knowing

"A lake is clearest when it is undisturbed. Likewise, the answers you seek will appear when your mind is still and your heart is open."

The Stream Within

"To flow is not to surrender control, but to remember you were never separate from the stream."

The Thorn and the Rose

"Jealousy is a thorn that does not wound the rose—it only pricks the hand that holds it."

The Wellspring Within

"All the rivers you have searched for outside — peace, love, freedom — were quietly flowing within you all along."

The Wisdom of Shadows

"Light reveals the world, but shadows reveal the soul. Do not fear your darkness—it is where transformation begins."

Unseen Roots

"Like a tree growing in stillness, your deepest growth is hidden—but it anchors everything that flowers."

"The River's Whisper

"True strength flows like a river—quiet, unyielding, and carving its path even through the hardest stone."

Shades of Existence

Light of life

"The light we seek is not outside of us, but within. It is the quiet brilliance of our spirit, revealing the truth that the brightest flame often begins as a single, humble spark."

- *Shree Shambav*

Awakened Deserving

"You don't manifest what you beg for; you manifest what you believe you already deserve."

Awakened Design

"You are not a visitor in this universe — you are its co-creator, encoded with the same essence that births galaxies."

Between Breath and Becoming

"In the space between one breath and the next, lies the power to choose a new karmic thread."

Beyond Reward and Punishment

"Neither karma nor manifestation are about deserving — they are about resonance. You don't get what you want. You get what you are."

Beyond the Curtain of Time

"Life is not a single story but a series of echoes, written in stars, carried by the winds of eternity."

Beyond the Horizon

"The journey is not about reaching a destination, but about dissolving the illusion of separation—awakening to the eternal oneness that has always been."

Divine Delay

"Delay is not denial—it is the universe preparing your miracle with the precision of sacred timing."

Echoes of the Inner Sky

"The universe is not testing you — it is reflecting you, amplifying the tone of your thoughts and the pulse of your emotions."

Echoes of the Unanswered

"In the silence of the unknown, we find the echo of our deepest questions—each unanswered mystery is not a void, but an invitation to explore, to expand, and to grow into a deeper connection with the infinite."

Fading Footprints

"We walk this world like waves upon the sand—vanishing, yet never truly gone."

Fire and Ashes

"We are not defined by what we have lost, but by how we rise from the ashes of our becoming."

Frequency of Truth

"Your vibration rises the moment your thoughts stop lying to your soul."

Hearts Speak Louder

"The heart's vibration is the soul's language—speak your desires not just with words, but with feeling."

In the Depths of Silence

"Some truths are too heavy for words, so they settle in the silence, waiting for a heart that listens."

Inner Weather

"You cannot control the storms of life, but you can choose the weather of your mind."

Karma as the Ink

"Your life is not written by fate, but by the ink of your awareness — karma is only the parchment."

Living in the Endless Unfolding

"In embracing the eternal, we are reminded that every moment is a reflection of something greater—our lives are not fleeting, but part of an endless unfolding that transcends time and space, carrying with it the essence of all that is."

Living with Awareness

"To prepare for the journey beyond is to live each day with awareness, to connect with the spirit, and to make peace with both the life we've lived and the mysteries that await us."

Love's Everlasting Presence

"Love is never truly lost; it simply changes its form—what was once a hand to hold may become the wind that whispers your name."

Love's Gentle Return

"Loss is not the end of love; it is its transformation. Like the tide that withdraws only to return, love finds its way back in unexpected waves."

Merging with the Divine

"To dissolve is not to disappear but to become everything—to return to the river, the wind, the endless sky."

Out of the Silence

"Even in the quiet, love sings. Even in the stillness, life moves. Even in the end, something begins."

Path of Sacred Repetition

"What repeats in your life is not a curse — it is a sacred invitation to meet yourself with new eyes."

Preparing for the Journey

"Preparing for the journey beyond is not about anticipating an end, but about embracing the unknown with the wisdom of a soul that has lived fully, loved deeply, and learned to let go."

Sacred Intention

"When intention rises from love rather than lack, it becomes a divine decree rather than a desperate plea."

Sacred Resistance

"Obstacles are not roadblocks—they are sacred signals asking, 'Are you ready to rise higher?'"

Sacred Surrender

"When you surrender control, you do not lose power—you merge with it."

Surrender to the Eternal Flow

"To embrace the eternal is to surrender to the timeless flow of existence, where the boundaries of life and death dissolve, and we realise that we are both part of the vastness and the stillness that precedes and follows every breath."

The Alchemy of Intention

"A single intention held with truth has more power than a thousand scattered desires."

The Alchemy of Intention

"When intention is pure, the universe conspires not in chaos, but in symphony — unseen threads weaving dreams into form."

The Art of Receiving

"Manifestation is less about force and more about becoming empty enough to receive the gifts already waiting in your name."

The Breath of Belonging

"To belong is not to fit into a world; it is to remember that the wind, the stars, the earth have always carried your imprint."

The Cosmic Conversation

"Life is not happening to you. It is speaking with you. Your thoughts are not echoes — they are invitations."

The Courage to Receive

"It takes great courage not just to ask—but to receive what your spirit has long whispered for."

The Creator's Awakening

"You are not waiting for the universe to change your life — the universe is waiting for you to remember you are its co-creator."

The Currency of Presence

"Time is not your greatest resource — attention is. Where your attention flows, your reality grows."

The Dance Beyond Fear

"When you lay down your fears, even for a moment, life begins to dance with you — not as an adversary, but as an ancient lover who never truly left."

The Dance of Destiny

"Destiny is not fixed. It is choreographed by the rhythm of your consciousness and the steps of your intention."

The Dance of Karma and Choice

"Karma does not punish — it teaches. And with awareness, every cycle becomes a chance to choose again."

The Dance of Time

"The past is a whisper, the future a dream, but the present is a dance. If you live too much in what was or what will be, you forget to move to the rhythm of now."

The Echo of Silence

"True wisdom is not found in the noise of knowledge, but in the silence of understanding—where the soul listens, and the universe speaks."

The Echo of the Infinite

"When you listen beyond words, beyond even silence, you will hear the echo of the infinite, calling you back to yourself."

The Energy of Enough

"The moment you decide you are enough, your entire vibration changes—and the world responds."

The Eternal Dialogue

"Every moment is a message. Every outcome is a mirror. And every experience is the universe answering the questions you didn't know you were asking."

The Eternal Echo of Love

"The ones we love may leave, but love itself is eternal. It finds new faces, new moments, and new ways to remind us it never really left."

The Eternal Unfolding

"The soul does not fear the unknown; it longs for it, for beyond the veil lies not an end, but the great unfolding of all that was, is, and will be."

The Fire That Heals

"True manifestation is not the fire that consumes, but the fire that purifies what no longer serves."

The Fire of Becoming

"You are not here to stay safe in your stories—you are here to set them on fire and walk through their ashes reborn."

The Garden of Intent

"Each thought you nurture is a seed. Each feeling you water is a bloom. Tend to your inner garden with sacred hands."

The Grace of Delay

"Not every closed door is denial; sometimes it is divine timing waiting for your readiness."

The Healing Path

"What breaks you open also clears the path for your light to pour through."

The Hearth of Stillness

"In the heart of stillness, you will not find emptiness — you will find the first fire from which all stars were born."

The Homecoming

"Enlightenment is not a journey outward, but the simplest homecoming to the place you never truly left."

The Invisible Thread

"Between every thought and every breath runs an invisible thread — when you hold it with awareness, life itself listens."

The Karma Within the Wish

"Every desire carries the echo of past actions. To manifest wisely is to harmonise your wish with your wisdom."

The Lament of the Moon

"Even the moon, bathed in borrowed light, still finds beauty in its quiet longing for the sun."

The Light We Leave Behind

"We do not live forever, but the love we give does. It lingers in the kindness we've shown, the lives we've touched, and the light we leave behind."

The Light Within

"A lamp does not seek the sun to shine—it burns from within. So must you. Do not wait for the world to light your path; become the flame that guides your own way."

The Light Within

"You are not seeking the light; you are only peeling away the layers of forgetting that once hid your own radiance."

The Mirror Within

"Your outer reality is merely the echo of the beliefs you whisper to yourself in silence."

The Mirror of Karma

"Karma does not judge — it reflects. What you plant in thought and action, it returns in experience."

The Mirror of the Cosmos

"The universe does not respond to your words — it echoes the silent vibrations of your consciousness."

The Mirror of the Infinite

"When you gaze into existence with a clear heart, you do not merely see the world — you see the infinite gazing back at you."

The Mirror of the Soul

"The world is a mirror, reflecting not what we see, but who we are. A kind soul finds beauty everywhere, while a restless heart sees only shadows."

The Mirror of the Soul

"We do not see the world as it is; we see it as we are. A pure heart finds beauty in darkness, while a clouded soul sees shadows even in the light."

The Music of Silence

"The heart's truest melodies are not composed of notes, but of the spaces between them—where longing, loss, and love intertwine in quiet harmony."

The Neutral Universe

"The universe is not a genie — it is a mirror. It magnifies what you believe, fear, and repeatedly choose."

The Ocean Within

"Every storm we survive leaves behind a deeper stillness, a vastness within that mirrors the sea."

The Peace of the Unknown

"In the face of the unknown, it is not the certainty of answers that brings peace, but the acceptance of the mystery itself, knowing that life's greatest wisdom often arises from embracing what cannot be understood."

The Power of Unanswered Questions

"The beauty of the infinite lies not in the answers we find, but in the questions that continue to awaken wonder, inviting us to explore deeper realms of mystery and truth."

The Power to Begin Again

"Karma may explain your story, but it never defines your ending. Consciousness holds the power to begin

The Pulse of Purpose

"When you align with your soul's purpose, even time bends to support your becoming."

The Pulse of the Universe

"Every note of music, every whisper of wind, every heartbeat is a thread in the infinite song of existence."

The Quiet Alchemy

"Transformation does not thunder; it whispers. It turns quietly, like the seasons, in the secret soil of your being."

The Quiet Architect

"Every thought you cradle, every emotion you nourish, is a blueprint gently laid upon the fabric of reality."

The Quiet Rebellion of Hope

"To hope is an act of quiet rebellion. It is to stand in the ruins of yesterday and still believe in the sunrise of tomorrow."

The Quiet Rewriting

"Every moment of mindfulness is a quiet rewriting of your destiny."

The Return to Wholeness

"Healing is not becoming something new; it is returning to the ancient, unbroken song you have always been."

The Sacred Mirror

"The world you see is but the reflection of the world you believe — polish the mirror of your heart, and the universe will shine back with wonder."

The Sacred Pause

"In the pause between desire and arrival lies your greatest test — will you fill it with fear, or fuel it with faith?"

The Sacred Pause

"Sometimes, it is not the next step that matters, but the sacred pause — where the universe reshapes itself around your stillness."

The Seed of Worthiness

"Plant the belief that you are already worthy, and you will harvest a life where love and abundance are the natural fruits."

The Silent Symphony

"True power is born not in noise, but in the silence that cradles every sound — where the heart remembers its song before it is sung."

The Song of the Departed

"No soul is ever lost, only carried by the wind, whispered through the stars, and written in the waves."

The Soul's Compass

"Purpose is not found in the noise of the world but in the quiet conviction that your life is meant to mean something more."

The Theatre of Existence

"We play our roles upon this stage, never knowing when the final curtain will fall—only that the story continues beyond the veil."

The Timeless Pulse

"Beneath the ticking of clocks and the racing of dreams, there is a pulse untouched by time — and it beats within you."

The Unfinished Symphony

"No song truly ends, for every note lingers in the spaces between—waiting to be heard again in another life, another time."

The Unseen Architecture

"The universe builds realities with the bricks of your intentions, mortar of your emotions, and blueprint of your soul."

The Voice of Eternity

"Silence is not the absence of sound, but the presence of truth—listen closely, and you will hear eternity speaking through the stillness of your soul."

The Weaver of Realities

"Your intention is the loom, your focus the thread — every thought you hold weaves another corner of the reality you live in."

The Weight of Light

"Even the brightest light has known the burden of darkness, and still, it chooses to shine."

The Weight of Unspoken Prayers

"What you refuse to feel, you will continue to repeat. Healing begins when silence meets truth."

The Wisdom in the Questions

"The journey through life and death is not defined by the answers we seek, but by the wisdom we cultivate in the questions we dare to ask, and the courage to embrace the mystery that lies beyond them."

The Witness Beyond Names

"You are not the story you tell yourself. You are the witness — the unnamable presence watching the river of names pass by."

Vibration Before Form

"Everything you wish to see in the outer world begins as a silent resonance within your inner field."

Vibration is the Invitation

"Every vibration you hold is an invitation—become what you seek, and it will come looking for you."

Where the Heart Belongs

"Home is not a place, but the feeling of being known, even in the vastness of the unknown."

Whispers of Eternity

"Beyond the echoes of time and memory, love lingers—not in the words spoken, but in the silence that remains when all else fades."

Wounds into Windows

"Your pain was never a punishment. It was a passage — a window into your depth, not your defect."

The Beauty of Simplicity

Embracing Life's Little Pleasures

"Simplicity is not the absence of richness, but the presence of clarity. It is in the quiet moments of stillness, the unspoken joys, that we uncover the profound beauty of life."

- *Shree Shambav*

A New One, A New Chance

"Life does not count your losses; it gifts you a 'new one' to rise, to heal, to love once more."

Bridges Over Blood

"Family isn't who shares your name, but who stands beside you when the world falls apart."

Closure's Paradox

"Closure is not the end of pain; it is the acceptance that some wounds will ache even as they heal."

Contentment in Simplicity

"Simplicity holds the key to a contented heart. When desires quiet, we realise that we need very little to experience profound happiness and peace."

Courage in Action

"True courage is not the absence of fear, but the willingness to act despite it."

Echoes of Kindness

"A single kind word can outlive lifetimes, whispered through generations in the wind of memory."

Embracing Mystery

"Seek not the answers to life's questions, but the wisdom to embrace its mysteries."

Faith in Bloom

"Even a single flower, blooming against the odds, can be proof that life is still on your side."

Freedom Beyond Attachment

"True freedom is not the absence of chains, but the release from attachment."

Imperfect Light

"Even in the cracks of who we were, the light of who we're becoming finds its way through."

Love Beyond Conditions

"True love transcends conditions, expectations, and judgments. It is a state of being that honours the divine presence within all life, seeing beyond the surface."

Love in the Quiet Moments

"Love is not measured by grand gestures but by the quiet moments of understanding, the unspoken support, and the willingness to grow together through life's trials and triumphs."

Nature's Sacred Symphony

"In the whisper of the wind and the rhythm of the waves lies a sacred symphony, reminding us that nature's quiet harmony is the music our souls long to hear."

Return to Existence

"A moment of pure stillness is not an escape, but a return to the heart of existence."

Roots That Hold

"Strength isn't in the absence of storms but in the roots that hold you steady when they rage."

Sacred Fracture

"Every sacred becoming begins with a beautiful fracture."

Shadows of Regret

"The loudest ghosts are not the ones that haunt you but the ones you carry within—the echoes of choices left unmade."

Shadows of the Soul

"The ghosts of our past do not haunt us to punish, but to remind us of the strength we gained when we faced them."

Silent Scars, Loud Strength

"Some battles leave scars no one sees, but it is in those unseen marks that resilience quietly blooms."

Stillness is a Door

"In the space between letting go and becoming, stillness opens the door to grace."

The Art of Letting Go

"Let go of all that doesn't bring you peace, for only in release will you find the doorway to true joy."

The Art of Listening

"The universe speaks in the language of joy; listen deeply, and it will guide your home."

The Art of Non-Attachment

"Non-attachment is not detachment but an active appreciation of each moment without the need to possess it. In letting go, we make space for divine abundance to flow."

The Beauty of Simplicity

"Joy is found in the simplest acts—breathing, watching, listening. When you embrace simplicity, the universe opens."

The Bridge of Love

"Love is the bridge we build when everything else fails—a testament to the bonds that defy time and blood."

The Compass of Joy

"When you are in joy, you are home. Every step in harmony with yourself brings you closer to the centre of all things."

The Cost of Ambition

"Ambition, when untethered, is a fire that burns bright but consumes the soul; it is the journey toward the peak, but not without leaving parts of yourself behind."

The Courage to Feel

"It takes more courage to feel your pain than to flee it—and therein lies your healing."

The Courage to Trust

"Faith is the courage to trust the unseen, to move forward without needing guarantees. It is a silent prayer whispered to the universe, believing that all will unfold as it should."

The Courage to Unfold

"There is no becoming without the courage to let who you were fall away."

The Dance of Creation

"In the dance of creation, the self is both the dancer and the rhythm, boundless and inseparable."

The Dance of Duality

"Life is a dance of opposites—joy and sorrow, love and loss, peace and conflict. Embracing this duality with equanimity is the path to true harmony within."

The Dance of Energy

"Life is energy flowing; when you block it with duty alone, it stagnates. Allow it to flow freely, and you come alive."

The Dawn of a New One

"Every 'new one' carries the whispers of endings and the promise of beginnings—an unwritten story waiting for your ink."

The Divine Flute

"Empty yourself of ego, and become a flute through which the divine breathes its eternal song—each note a whisper of love, each melody a call to unity."

The Echo of the Past

"The past is a shadow that follows us, not out of malice, but to remind us of who we were, so we may decide who we will become."

The Ego's Dissolution

"When the ego dissolves, the soul awakens to its timeless truth: that it was always one with all."

The Essence of Solace

"If solace were tangible, it would rest in your essence, the unspoken language of understanding that wraps around the heart like a quiet, reassuring whisper."

The Eternal Quest for Wisdom

"Knowledge is gathered, but wisdom is revealed through experience and introspection. It is the deep understanding that arises from the soul's journey."

The Flow of Existence

"To be in flow is to be in tune with the universe, each moment a quiet song of alignment and grace."

The Fragile Thread

"Life hangs by a thread so fine, we often mistake it for indestructible rope—until it snaps, and we are left holding the frayed ends, searching for meaning in the loss."

The Freedom of Choice

"Choose only what brings you joy, and you will feel freedom. Every other choice is a prison we build around our spirit."

The Frequency of Love

"Every moment you align with love, you tune yourself to the frequency of the divine."

The Gift of Presence

"The present moment is a gift wrapped in layers of timelessness. Unwrap it, and life unfolds in its truest form."

The Gift of Stillness

Stillness is not the absence of movement but the fullness of presence."

The Grace of Humility

"Humility is the quiet strength that allows us to be open to learning. It is the grace to acknowledge our limitations, making space for the divine wisdom to enter."

The Grace of Stopping

"In stopping, we discover what truly moves us. In silence, we find the rhythm of our true heartbeat."

The Heart's Bridge

"The heart is the bridge between the finite and the infinite; to walk it is to remember your eternal nature."

The Heart's True North

"The heart is a compass—sometimes, it leads us through storms and darkness, but it always knows the way back to what is true."

The Hollow Reed

"When you silence the noise of the mind, you become the hollow reed through which the universe weaves its infinite harmony."

The Illusion of Control

"We live under the illusion of control, as though we can master time and fate, but the truth is we only control how we respond to the winds of change."

The Inner Sanctuary

"The most sacred place is the inner sanctuary of the heart, where the soul rests in communion with the divine. Here, we find the peace that transcends all understanding."

The Inward Path

"The path to divinity is not a journey outward but an unfolding inward, where the infinite resides."

The Language of Connection

"True connection is found in the spaces between words, where hearts speak a language of trust, compassion, and the courage to embrace each other's imperfections."

The Light Within

"True wealth is the glow in your heart when you do what you love, for the world's richest treasures lie within."

The Mind's Place

"The mind is a servant; it only becomes the master when we lose sight of who we truly are."

The Mirror of Truth

"When you look inward with joy, the world reflects peace. The mirror of your soul holds the image of all creation."

The Mirror of the Present

"The present is the mirror where your past reflects and your future takes form."

The Nature of Wholeness

"Wholeness is not a destination; it is the feeling of being centred. When you are whole, you are already where you need to be."

The Ocean of Serenity

"Dive into the ocean of your inner joy. Only there will you find the stillness that nothing can disturb."

The Path of Inner Light

"Your centre is not just a place; it is a light, guiding you through life's shadows with a gentle, unshakable warmth."

The Pathless Path

"The soul does not walk a straight line—it spirals, it sheds, and it sings its way home."

The Pathless Path

"The soul does not walk a straight line—it spirals, it sheds, and it sings its way home."

The Power of Enjoyment

"Joy is not a luxury; it is a compass. When you follow what lights you up, you move closer to the truth of who you are."

The Power of Unspoken Words

"There are conversations held in the spaces between words, in the glances, in the pauses, in the things we choose not to say, and yet they speak volumes."

The Power of Words

"Words are seeds—once sown, they take root in hearts, shaping destinies in silence."

The Price of Love

"Love is not the easy choice, nor the safest; it is a treasure dug from the deepest caverns of the soul, sometimes won only through sacrifice."

The Quiet Rebirth

"Transformation doesn't always roar—it often whispers from the softest part of you."

The Radiance of Being

"When you connect with your centre, even in silence, you radiate more light than a thousand suns."

The Redemption of Silence

"In the end, silence doesn't speak louder than words; it begs for them, craving the honesty that could have been."

The Sacred Current

"You do not need to push the river—just remember that you are made of its current."

The Shape of Trust

"Trust is not built from knowing the path—it is born from walking it anyway."

The Silence of the Soul

"In silence, you find the whispers of the soul. In those whispers, you find everything you need to know."

The Sky Was Listening

"On certain nights, the stars don't just shine—they witness. And in their gaze, even silence becomes a sacred prayer."

The Soul's Canvas

"Your thoughts shape your world, but your soul shapes your thoughts."

The Soul's Motion

"The soul was never meant to stay still—its truth is revealed only through motion."

The Strength in Vulnerability

"To be strong is not to stand tall in silence but to kneel in honesty and say, 'I cannot carry this alone.'"

The Symphony of Life

"Life is not a battle to be won but a symphony to be harmonised, where every note matters."

The Symphony of Stillness

"Surrender to stillness and let the divine play its symphony through you—unseen hands crafting timeless beauty in every moment."

The Tapestry of Life

"The earth speaks in colours, textures, and scents, weaving a tapestry of life that invites us to pause, breathe, and remember that we, too, are part of its endless song."

The Torch of Legacy

"A legacy is not the gold we leave behind, but the fire we kindle in the hearts of those who come after us, a fire that illuminates their path when our own light has dimmed."

The Unbreakable Spirit

"The spirit of the awakened soul remains unbreakable. No outer force can bend what is rooted in the divine, for it knows itself beyond the confines of the physical."

The Unfolding Self

"You are not becoming someone else—you're unwrapping the truth that was always within you."

The Wealth of Contentment

"Contentment is the richest state of being; it is the quiet assurance that everything you need is within."

The Weight of Goodbye

"A father's final words are not a request; they are a legacy passed into trembling hands."

The Weight of Holding On

"Holding on can feel like carrying the world, but it also means refusing to let go of the people who make that weight worthwhile."

The Weight of Love

"True love is not measured by the ease of its journey, but by the weight it carries through storms and still chooses to endure."

The Weight of Regret

"Regret is a stone that sits heavy in your chest, pressing down with every breath, yet teaching you the value of choices you never knew you had."

The Weight of Regret

"Regret isn't the burden of the past; it's the unspoken truth waiting for the courage of a single moment."

The Weight of Silence

"Sometimes, the loudest moments are not those filled with words, but those where silence holds you captive, waiting for something you cannot yet name."

The Weight of Silence

"Unspoken words weigh heavier than those spoken in haste—choose silence only when it heals, not when it wounds."

The Weight of a New One

"A 'new one' is not just a fresh start—it is a responsibility to be braver, wiser, and truer than before."

The Wisdom Within

"Wisdom is not accumulated knowledge, but the quiet realisation that all you seek is already within you."

The Wisdom of Detachment

"Do not cling to actions you do not love; they pull you away from your centre. Let go, and feel yourself return."

The Wisdom of Joy

"In joy lies wisdom, for it is only in joy that we can touch the truth that all things are one."

Thread of Light

"Every conscious act untangles a karmic knot and weaves a new thread in the fabric of your becoming."

Truth Beyond Thought

"What intellect alone cannot reach, surrender often touches in silence."

Weightless in Change

"Change does not ask you to carry more—it invites you to release what was never yours."

When the Stars Bear Witness

"Under a sky that listens, even our most hidden wounds find the courage to speak."

Whispers of Eternity

"To listen deeply is to hear the whispers of eternity in the echoes of the present."

Life Coach and Philanthropist

Shree Shambav is the visionary founder of the Shree Shambav Ayur Rakshita Foundation (www.shambav-ayurrakshita.org). He founded this institution with a lofty goal: to recognise human identity across gender, ethnicity, and nationality. Through this organisation, he wants to assist all communities in realising their full potential and the intrinsic beauty of life.

Shree Shambav, a Life Coach, is dedicated to supporting people on their journeys of self-discovery and empowerment. He assists people in discovering who they are, determining what inspires and drives them, and overcoming limiting ideas. His approach clarifies what one wants in life, assisting people through goal-setting and a step-by-step process for achieving them. He empowers people to make deliberate and responsible decisions, allowing them to identify their blind spots and evolve as individuals via the use of numerous strategies and tools.

The foundation's bold, uncompromising, and compassionate ventures are always aimed at initiating the "Inner Transformation" process. They focus on spiritual growth, personal growth, and self-healing while emphasising that true progress lies in "Inclusive Growth and Co-existence." This philosophy drives all their initiatives, encouraging a holistic approach to development and well-being.

Under Shree Shambav's leadership, the foundation has launched several impactful movements:

Shree Shambav Green Movement: This mission is to create a healthy, green, and clean earth through responsible water conservation and greening initiatives. The movement strives to make the world a green paradise by encouraging sustainable living and environmental responsibility.

Shree Shambav Vidya Vedhika (Vizhuthugal): This project aims to help students and children by offering training, books, stationery, and uniforms. It aims to provide the next generation with the tools and resources they need to excel both academically and personally.

Shree Shambav and his foundation exemplify the spirit of compassion, transformation, and inclusive growth via their work, which has a profound impact on individuals and communities around the world. His work exemplifies the power of acknowledging and nourishing the human spirit, creating a world in which everyone can reach their full potential and appreciate the beauty of life.

TESTIMONIALS

Journey of Soul - Karma - "We die in our twenties and are buried at eighty." Remember that nothing can stop someone who refuses to be stopped. "Most people do not fail; they simply give up." Shree Shambav deserves full credit. It allowed me to sit and consider what I might miss out on in life. The author has delved into every aspect of our daily lives. How can a seemingly insignificant change in these seemingly insignificant details bring us such joy? The Soul of Journey teaches you the "art of living" as well as the "art of dying."

Twenty + One Series - The rich cultural heritage offered a host of twenty + one short stories with incredible imagination, morals and values prevalent at a given time, influencing how people respond to a crisis or any situation. The author has recreated images with universal values and morals. The plentiful of fascinating from faraway lands would leave the modern play and story writers a cringe. The book supports trust and immeasurable values, instilling hope for the new generations.

Death - "Shree Shambav's 'Death - Light of Life and the Shadow of Death' is an extraordinary masterpiece that delves deep into the profound questions surrounding our existence and mortality. The book's opening statement, 'Nothing ever truly dies; it simply ceases to exist in one form before resuming it in another,' sets the stage for a thought-provoking exploration of death's multifaceted nature. Shambav's remarkable ability to navigate the philosophical complexities of death and our universal fear of it is both enlightening and comforting. This book is a testament to the power of understanding and acceptance."

Whispers of Eternity - "Reading 'Whispers of Eternity' by Shree Shambav was a transformative experience that left me captivated from beginning to end. Each section of this exquisite collection delves into the myriad facets of existence, offering poignant reflections on life, death, and everything in between. Shree Shambav's verses are a testament to the beauty of language and the power of expression, inviting readers to embark on a journey of self-discovery and spiritual awakening. Whether celebrating life's simple joys or grappling with the complexities of human emotion, this book is a timeless companion that speaks to the heart and soul of every reader."

Life Changing Journey Series - "Life Changing Journey Series II Inspirational Quotes" is a remarkable collection that illuminates the path to self-discovery and personal growth. With its inspiring quotes and insightful reflections, this book serves as a beacon of light in a world often shrouded in darkness. Each quote offers wisdom, guidance, and encouragement, reminding readers of their inner strength and resilience. A must-read for anyone seeking inspiration and enlightenment.

Learn To Love Yourself – "A Heartfelt Guide to Authentic Self-Love." "Learn to Love Yourself" invites readers on a transformative journey to embrace their true essence in a world often focused on external validation. Through ten insightful chapters, it gently reveals principles of genuine self-love, guiding readers to deepen their connection with themselves. Beyond surface positivity, it encourages the cultivation of resilient self-acceptance, from embracing one's unique qualities to setting empowering boundaries. With inspiring stories and practical wisdom, this book is a trusted companion on the path to inner peace, fulfilment, and joy, helping readers build lives that reflect their authentic selves.

The Power of Letting Go – This book has been a gift to my spiritual journey. Shree Shambav's insights into attachment, personal growth cycles, and forgiveness are enlightening. The concept of seven-year cycles resonated with me, helping me understand the natural phases of life. I feel more empowered to let go of what no longer serves me and step into a life of freedom and fulfilment. A truly beautiful read!

A Journey of Lasting Peace – "A Journey of Lasting Peace" feels like a trusted friend guiding you through the maze of self-discovery. The 18 transformative principles are both practical and deeply resonant, addressing everything from gratitude practices to the art of letting go. Each chapter is infused with warmth and wisdom, making it easy to apply the concepts to my life. I particularly appreciated the emphasis on physical health's connection to mental well-being; it served as a wake-up call for me to prioritise my health. This book is an invaluable resource for anyone serious about personal growth!

Astrology Unveiled Series – "Profound, Logical, and Inspiring". What stands out in Astrology Unveiled is the author's dedication to making Vedic astrology logical and approachable. Each concept flows naturally into the next, backed by examples and exercises. The insights into karma and life cycles add a philosophical depth rarely seen in astrology books. Perfect for anyone seeking spiritual growth alongside astrological knowledge!

The Entitlement Trap - "Thought-Provoking and Challenging" The book challenges readers to confront their own sense of entitlement, and that's not easy—but it's essential. The Entitlement Trap doesn't offer a one-size-fits-all approach. Instead, it's a thoughtful, layered examination of how entitlement can limit our growth. The chapter on "Defining Your Own Hill" was particularly impactful, as it pushed me to reconsider which challenges are truly worth pursuing. A thought-provoking read for those willing to do the inner work to create a life they can be proud of.

Whispers of a Dying Soul – "A Soul-Stirring Reflection on Life's Unspoken Truths" - *Whispers of a Dying Soul: Unspoken Regrets and Unlived Dreams"* is a deeply moving exploration of the unexpressed emotions and unfulfilled aspirations that shape our lives in ways we often don't realise. This book invites readers to confront the powerful, often hidden impact of regret while guiding them through a journey of introspection and healing. Each page opens a space to reflect on the choices that define us—from moments of unspoken love to neglected passions—offering a gentle reminder to live authentically and courageously.

Whispers of the Soul: A Journey Through Haiku - is a mesmerising collection that speaks directly to the heart. Each haiku is a delicate brushstroke capturing life's fleeting beauty and timeless wisdom, inviting readers into moments of deep reflection and peace. This book is a balm for the soul, guiding us to find meaning in stillness and connection in simplicity. The themes of nature, love, and mindfulness echo universal truths, resonating with quiet, powerful grace. It's a book to be savoured slowly, cherished deeply, and returned to often. Truly, it is a gift for anyone seeking calm and clarity in life's chaos.

Whispers of Silence - Unlocking Inner Power through Stillness by Shree Shambav is a rare gem that beckons readers to pause, reflect, and reconnect with their inner selves. In a world that never stops talking, this book offers a profound exploration of silence—not as a void but as a rich and transformative space.

From the first page, Shree Shambav's writing resonates deeply, blending scientific insights with spiritual wisdom in a way that feels both universal and deeply personal. The author's ability to bridge the tangible and the transcendent makes this book an invaluable guide for anyone navigating the chaos of modern life.

The Power of Words: Transforming Speech, Transforming Lives - The Power of Words is a profound and enlightening guide that has transformed the way I approach communication. Shree Shambav masterfully uncovers the hidden influence of our words on relationships, self-perception, and overall well-being. This book doesn't just teach you how to speak; it inspires mindful communication that fosters connection and trust. The insights on replacing negative patterns like gossip and judgment with kindness and authenticity are truly life-changing. The practical strategies and engaging narratives make it an invaluable resource for personal and professional growth. A must-read for anyone striving to communicate with intention, clarity, and compassion. Highly recommended!

The Art of Intentional Living: Minimalism for a Life of Purpose - "The Art of Intentional Living is a refreshing guide to finding clarity in a cluttered world. With practical wisdom and profound insights, it inspires you to simplify, prioritise, and live with purpose. A must-read for anyone seeking balance and fulfilment."

Awakening the Infinite: The Power of Consciousness in Transforming Life - "Awakening the Infinite is a transformative guide that expands the mind and nourishes the soul. With profound insights and practical wisdom, this book beautifully explores the power of consciousness, helping readers connect with their true purpose and inner potential. It is a journey of self-discovery, healing, and spiritual awakening, offering clarity and inspiration at every turn. A must-read for anyone looking to live with greater awareness, meaning, and authenticity."

Beyond the Veil: A Journey Through Life After Death:

"This book touched me in ways few others have—it's not just about death, but about life, meaning, and the vast unknown that connects them. Beyond the Veil offers a graceful blend of science and spirit, inviting us to explore the mystery with awe rather than fear. The stories, insights, and reflections linger in your heart long after the final page. A truly transformative read that brings light to the shadows of mortality. It reminded me that in embracing death, we truly learn how to live."

Bonds Beyond Blood:

"A profoundly moving story that reminds us family is not defined by blood, but by love, sacrifice, and the courage to heal. Every chapter touched my soul with its emotional truth and timeless wisdom. Through joy, grief, and redemption, this book captures the raw beauty of human connection. I saw reflections of my own family in its pages—both the pain and the hope. A powerful, unforgettable read that lingers long after the final word."

A Journey into Spiritual Maturity: 12 Golden Rules for Inner Transformation

"This book is a gentle yet powerful guide that awakened a deeper sense of purpose within me. Each golden rule felt like a mirror reflecting truths I needed to embrace. Shree Shambav's wisdom is timeless, poetic, and profoundly grounding. It's not just a read—it's a journey into the heart of who you truly are. A must-read for anyone seeking lasting peace, clarity, and inner transformation."

The Inner Battlefield: Overcoming the Enemies of the Mind and Soul:

"This book is a powerful revelation—an honest mirror to the battles we fight within. Every chapter is a step closer to clarity, peace, and emotional mastery. Shree Shambav brilliantly transforms ancient wisdom into practical guidance for modern souls. It awakened in me a new strength to face my fears and rise above inner turmoil. A must-read for anyone seeking true inner victory and lasting transformation."

The Seeker's Gold – Unlocking Life's Greatest Treasure

The Seeker's Gold is a soul-stirring masterpiece that goes far beyond the pursuit of wealth—it is a journey into the heart of what truly matters. Each chapter unfolds with poetic wisdom and emotional depth, revealing that life's real treasure is not found in riches but in the transformation of the self. As the protagonist evolves through trials, love, and profound realizations, so does the reader. This book is a mirror for every dreamer, a lantern for every seeker, and a companion for anyone walking the path of purpose. A timeless tale that stays with you long after the final page.

ACKNOWLEDGEMENTS

To my grandfathers, grandmothers, mothers, fathers, aunts, uncles, neighbours, sisters, brothers, friends, and teachers, they poured in endless moral stories, retellings of Ramayana, Mahabharata, Puranas, Upanishads, and so on.

My teachers, neighbours, and kindred souls. Who provided us with a stage to perform wonderful Puranic stories and were gracious enough to acknowledge our efforts.

The artists and translators of epics have served as a source of inspiration, invigorating our spirits, making these works accessible, and enabling us to grasp the profound depths and deeper dimensions they contain.

I also cherish the stimulating conversations I had with my wonderful mothers, Punitha Muniswamy and Uma Devi.

Our family's youngest member, Aadhya, who always overwhelmed me with questions, inspired this book.

I would likewise prefer to express gratitude to Mr Sivakumar, Mrs Roopa Sivakumar, Mr Akshaya

Rajesh, Ms Akshatha Rajesh, Ms Apeksha Prabhu, Mr Akanksh Prabhu, Mr Nikash Sarasambi, Mrs Spoorthi Nikash for their valuable inputs.

I must thank Mr Rajesh, Mr Savan Prabhu, Mrs Revathi Rajesh, Mrs Rajani Sarasambi, and Mrs Manju Reshma, who encouraged me and often suggested writing a book. Their unwavering belief that I had something valuable to offer kept me going during my writing sessions.

Love you all,

Shree Shambav

www.shambav.org

shreeshambav@gmail.com

www.ingramcontent.com/pod-product-compliance
Lightning Source LLC
LaVergne TN
LVHW091710070526
838199LV00050B/2343